DOG
LEADS TO
GOD

Other books by Henry Martin
to help you on your spiritual path:

The Dog Walker's Guide to God
52 musings on companionship, Divine and canine

Contains 52 five-minute-reads to inspire dog walkers to ponder the mysteries of faith and the wonders of God.

Vincent van Gogh and The Good Samaritan
The wounded painter's journey

A unique spiritual study of van Gogh's painting and the famous parable told by Jesus of Nazareth, bringing an uplifting new perspective to both.

Eavesdropping
Learning to pray from those who talked to Jesus

Suitable for daily reading and reflection during Lent, or any time of year, this book listens in on Jesus' conversations recorded in the gospels and asks, 'How does this help us with prayer today?'

Alongside
Reflections on Jesus' struggles and how he meets us in our struggles

Suitable for daily reading and reflection during Lent, or any time of year, this book considers the Gospel accounts of times that Jesus struggled and how his experiences can help us today.

For more information go to www.dltbooks.com

52 Divine Lessons from your Canine

HENRY MARTIN

INTELLIGENT ♦ INSPIRATIONAL ♦ INCLUSIVE
SPIRITUAL BOOKS

First published in 2025 by
Darton, Longman and Todd Ltd
Unit 1, The Exchange
6 Scarbrook Road
Croydon CR0 1UH
editorial@darton-longman-todd.co.uk

This product conforms to the requirements of the
European Union's General Product Safety Regulations (GPSR).
EU Authorised Representative for GPSR:
Easy Access System Europe –
Mustamäe tee 50, 10621 Tallinn, Estonia
gpsr.requests@easproject.com

© 2025 Henry Martin

The right of Henry Martin to be identified as the Author of this
work has been asserted in accordance with the Copyright,
Designs and Patents Act 1988.

ISBN: 978-1-915412-83-6

No part of this book may be used or reproduced in any manner for the
purpose of training artificial intelligence technologies or systems.

A catalogue record for this book is available from the British Library.

Designed and produced by Judy Linard

Printed and bound in India by Replika Press Pvt. Ltd.

This book is dedicated to all those generous souls who adopt senior dogs.

CONTENTS

INTRODUCTION	9
PART 1: LETTING THE NEWS HOUNDS LEAD YOU TO GOD	11
1. Ulysse: the updated parable	13
2. Cecil: dirty money and divine mercy	16
3. Rinka: never kick a pup	19
PART 2: LETTING YOUR DOG LEAD YOU THROUGH THE LORD'S PRAYER	21
4. Our Father in heaven	23
5. Hallowed be your name	26
6. Your kingdom come, on earth as in heaven	29
7. Your will be done, on earth as in heaven	32
8. Give us today our daily bread	34
9. Forgive us our sins	36
10. As we forgive those who sin against us	39
11. Lead us not into temptation	42
12. Deliver us from evil (i)	45
13. Deliver us from evil (ii)	47
14. For the Kingdom, the power and the glory are yours, for ever and ever, Amen	49
PART 3: LETTING YOUR DOG LEAD YOU THROUGH THE CHRISTIAN YEAR	51
15. Advent: the Second Coming	53
16. Advent: John the Baptist	55
17. Advent: staying awake, keeping alert	58
18. Christmas Eve	60
19. Christmas Day	62
20. Epiphany (the feast)	65
21. Epiphany (the season)	68
22. Lent	71
23. Maundy Thursday	74

THE DOG WALKER'S GUIDE TO GOD

24. Good Friday	77
25. Easter Sunday	80
26. Ascension	82
27. Pentecost	85
28. Ordinary Time	87

PART 4: LETTING YOUR DOG PACK LEAD YOU TO GOD — 91

29. It is not good for the dog to be alone	93
30. There is power in the union (or 'the pack')	96
31. Dogs do diversity	99
32. Accepting dogs as dogs	101
33. Ape kindness vs wolf kindness	104
34. The best pack in town (for dogs)	107
35. When the pack needs a reshuffle	110
36. What becomes of the broken hounds	113

PART 5: LETTING YOUR DOG'S TRAINING LEAD YOU TO GOD — 117

37. 'It's for your own good'	119
38. Steadiness	122
39. Helping your dog to grow in 'steadiness'	125
40. Little and often	128
41. Distractions	131
42. Nosetime: how much is too much?	134

PART 6: LETTING DOG WORK LEAD YOU TO GOD — 137

43. Finding food is work … wolf work	139
44. Walks are work … wolf work (i)	142
45. Walks are work … wolf work (ii)	145

PART 7: LETTING SOMETHING SAID ABOUT DOGS LEAD YOU TO GOD — 149

46. 'He's never done that before'	151
47. 'Will you STOP barking!'	154
48. 'You're supposed to be in control!'	156
49. 'You have everything you need! And yet you still want more?'	159
50. 'You're so brave … hiding behind that fence'	161
51. 'I wear my heart on a lead'	163

PART 8: TAIL ENDS — 167

52. Tail ends	169

CONCLUSION: CAN OUR DOGS LEAD US TO GOD? — 173
ACKNOWLEDGEMENTS — 175

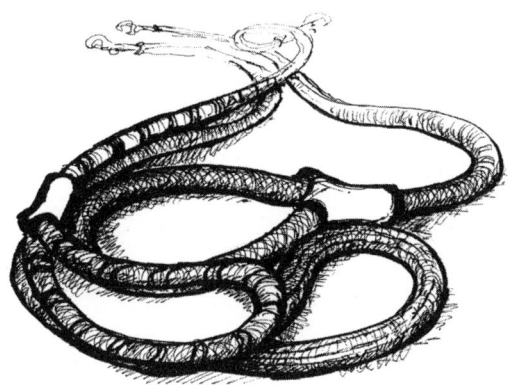

INTRODUCTION

If you share your home with a dog, you'll know already how they teach you about life *and* about yourself. But about God? How would that work? Dogs are neither preachers nor theologians, but maybe they can lead us to God, simply by being themselves whilst living cheek by jowl alongside us. We share the same Creator but we are also very different: our last common ancestor lived approximately 90–100 million years ago[1] and since then we have diverged. They kept all four paws on the ground. They are better at joie de vivre. We stand upright and have more refined ways of greeting our fellows.

This book's starting point is recognising that we, as humans have some 'God-like' duties towards our dogs. Take verses 7 and 8 from Psalm 121:

> The Lord will keep you from all evil;
> he will keep your life.
> The Lord will keep

---

[1] By comparison our last common ancestor with chimpanzees lived approximately 8–6 million years ago (according to the Smithsonian Institute)

THE DOG WALKER'S GUIDE TO GOD

>your going out and your coming in
>from this time on and for evermore. [2]

Now imagine your dog reciting this. Read it again in their voice, only this time swapping 'The Lord' for your name. It's a reasonable description of what our dogs should expect of us. Even if not a perfect fit, there is enough here to get us going, observing how we relate to our dogs and then flipping the scene around to ask, 'is that how God relates to us?'

The Bible's writers often employed a thought process called '*qal wahomer*'; (literally, 'light and heavy'). It depends on the following logic: 'if this small thing is true, then how much more will this much bigger thing also be true?' Jesus himself found it useful. It was also the basis of this book's companion, 'The Dog Walker's Guide to God'. The book you currently hold in your hands is not a sequel (so no worries if you have not read the other one … but please do!). It stands on its own and my hope is that as you read each daily section the life you share with your dog will enrich your life with God and vice versa.

Henry Martin,
Spring 2025

P.S. Dog guardians are usually convinced that their own dogs outrank and outperform all others. I stand guilty of this charge. And I have tried to compensate by making this book about more than our two but since they are the starting point for all my current dog to human, human to God observations, I'll take this opportunity to introduce them:

HUGO: rescued in 2021 as a two-year-old, is an occasionally reactive, oversized black Labrador lookalike with Beauceron and possibly Great Dane genes. He arrived with some trauma and very little experience of human affection. He has silky smooth fur and a lovely nature (even more so when he's calm).

HERA: rescued in 2023 as a three-year-old, she is also a black Labrador lookalike with maybe some terrier in there too. She is extremely sweet natured with humans, a ferocious playmate with other dogs and a shameless stealer of food.

[2] This and all subsequent quotes from the Bible are taken from the NRSVA.

PART 1

LETTING THE NEWS HOUNDS LEAD YOU TO GOD

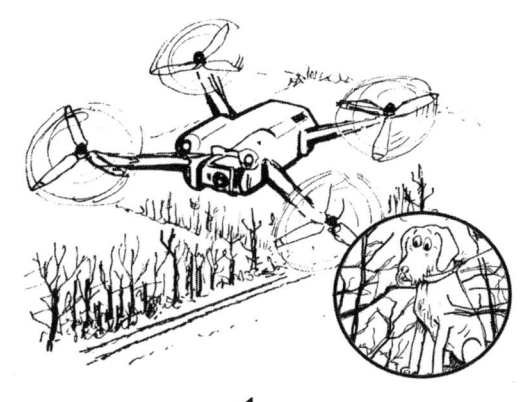

1
ULYSSE: THE UPDATED PARABLE

Ulysse's story was reported by the BBC in early January 2024 and resulted in a GoFundMe campaign that raised over £17,000.[3]

What a nightmare! Imagine being out on a walk. You turn around and your dog that just a moment ago was behind you, is nowhere to be seen. How long do you stay in the same place, waiting for your dog to return? How much calling do you do? How impotent do you feel? At what point do you decide to return home and hope that your dog will make their own way back?

This was the dilemma facing Sam Boyles when Ulysse, her wirehaired Hungarian Vizsla went missing. Just before Christmas they were out walking together in the countryside when Ulysse disappeared. Sam was frantic. Friends pitched in but no matter how hard they searched they could not find him. She refused to give up even after twelve long days had passed.

And then someone found him, still alive. That 'someone' was the pilot of an airborne thermal imaging camera, flown by the

---

[3] *Houghton Conquest lost dog found by thermal drone,* Danny Fullbrook and Andy Collins, BBC News, Bedfordshire, 6/1/2024

DOG LEADS TO GOD

charity Drone to Home. Their mission is to find lost dogs using drones. Their slogan states, 'We don't judge. We just reunite'. Two hours after their search began, they spotted a heat signature. They pinpointed the location and Sam went in, finding a thin, bedraggled but delighted Ulysse. His retractable lead had become entangled in a bush, trapping him completely. Once he was safely home and recovering, Sam set about fundraising for the charity.

In many ways this is just an update of a parable Jesus told two thousand years ago. Details differ in that Jesus' story features a shepherd and a missing sheep and lacks both drone and thermal imaging camera ... but otherwise the story is the same. A guardian searches and searches until the lost is found and then, in gratitude does something lavish to celebrate.

And if this shepherd is like God, then God is not as per some earlier versions, certainly not the Grumpy Greek God who sits on a throne in the clouds, thunderbolts ready to hand, itching to zap anyone foolish enough to displease him. Also not like God the cook who mixed some ingredients at the start of creation and then stepped back to snooze, waiting for the grand oven ping at the end of time to reveal what has risen and what has failed. Jesus' God is a distillation of different imagery found in the Hebrew Scriptures with an added and unexpected level of personal involvement: a God who welcomes small children and notices everything, even the number of hairs on a human head.[4] This God enters into human history, most notably by sending Jesus the Good Shepherd to seek and save the lost. This God is like: a woman who sweeps her entire house until a lost coin is found; a Dad who does not stop scanning the horizon as he awaits his reckless son's return and a Samaritan who stops to rescue a half-dead stranger from the gutter.[5] And like Drones to Home, this God seems far more interested in reuniting than in judging.

Because we love our dogs, we will go to extreme lengths to find them when they get lost. According to Jesus, God feels the same about us ... only more so.

[4] Matthew 19:13-14 and Luke 12:6-7
[5] Luke 15:1-31 and Luke 10:30-35

ULYSSE: THE UPDATED PARABLE

Something to chew as your dog walks alongside you
Can I comprehend that God loves me even more than I love my dog?

CECIL: DIRTY MONEY AND DIVINE MERCY

Like Ulysse, Cecil also went viral in January 2024. Cecil is a Doodle. His guardians needed cash for a new fence. They left an envelope containing $4000 on the sideboard in their kitchen. Cecil never steals, not even meat but every rule has an exception and on this day he ate the money. All of it. Some he just chewed up, some he ate up and then threw up leaving the remainder gone ... but not forever. After the requisite time, it reappeared crumpled, torn, chewed and ... erm .... coated. The bank offered to replace every note which had an intact serial number, so Cecil's guardians began the murky task of washing and piecing together the world's smelliest jigsaw puzzle. Incredibly they managed to salvage $3550, leaving the bill for Cecil's meal at just $450. Cecil was fine throughout the whole process.[6]

There are a couple of points to make about this story. First of all, humans and dogs may share the same home whilst living in very different worlds. Money, which is so valuable to humans, remains

[6] *This Pittsburgh couple's dog ate $4,000 but they got almost all of it back*, Ali Trachta, Pittsburgh City Paper, 14/12/2023

CECIL: DIRTY MONEY AND DIVINE MERCY

incomprehensible to dogs. If dogs had words they might argue, 'You humans! You forbid us many basic canine instincts and then get all fussy over some chewed up bits of paper!'

Then secondly we turn to God; would God do for us, what Cecil's guardians did for him? Would God clean up after us? Could God be that understanding and patient with us?

God's forbearance is remarkable. When we feel under attack, our instinct is to force our opponent to back off by whatever means possible. Jesus however, even as he was being killed, refused to threaten or even damn his oppressors. His prayer was, 'Father, forgive them; for they do not know what they are doing.'[7] Just as Cecil could never comprehend the financial cost of his snack so Jesus' crucifiers were not able to appreciate the magnitude of their crime. And so in both cases the godly option is to have mercy, generously accepting that someone you love finds themselves in a situation far beyond their capacity to understand.

As for the cleaning up, does God do anything for us which is analogous to Cecil's guardians sifting through his poo for chewed up bank notes? In one sense we, like Cecil will never know, just as we remain unaware of the times God protects us from unseen harm. There are some hints, however. The waiting Father, embraces his prodigal son, letting love override the stench of pigs.[8] Jesus gets hands-on in a smelly clean-up operation, one mealtime when no one else volunteers to wash the others' feet. By the time Jesus reaches Peter, he reveals a greater purpose than that evening's required podal refreshing. There is a far deeper cleansing of a far more engrained dirt that he alone can bring; should Peter shun this, it will be at his peril. Jesus put it like this, 'Unless I wash you, you have no share with me',[9] surely a reference to his forthcoming crucifixion, an act of service even more malodourously unpleasant than Cecil's guardians' task.

Paul has a more sanitised take, claiming, 'We know that all things work together for good for those who love God',[10] which could also mean that God works beyond our senses, tidying up

[7] Luke 23:24
[8] Luke 15:11-32
[9] John 13:8
[10] Romans 8:28

some messes of which we are unaware and bringing unexpected blessings to boot. We might recoil from the reek of our errors, both culpable and unintentional; mercifully God does not.

 Something to chew as your dog walks alongside you
How much can we know of God's merciful patience and how much can we guess at what we do not know?

Rinka
died October 1975
whose death was witnessed by God (from whom no secrets are hid)

3
RINKA: NEVER KICK A PUP

Rinka is our third hound who made the news. Sadly, unlike the previous two, this is a cautionary tale rather than a happy one. Rinka, a young Great Dane was murdered in October 1975 on the orders of Jeremy Thorpe, MP and rising star pipped for PM. He had nothing against Rinka herself; she was merely collateral waste. Thorpe's actual target was Rinka's owner, Norman Scott a vulnerable young man who to this day maintains that Thorpe raped him. Thorpe denied any sexual contact but all the same sought to 'cleanse' the past by engaging the services of a hit man. He is quoted as saying, 'We've got to get rid of him [Scott]. It is no worse than shooting a sick dog.'[11]

Thorpe's hired man took Scott to a deserted moorland spot in Somerset. Rinka sadly got in the way. Scott survived and was later found by an AA patrolman, sobbing beside her dead body.

… 'no worse than *shooting a sick dog*'. Hmmm … some phrases reveal much about their speaker. How we treat dogs can be indicative

---

[11] 'It is no worse than shooting a sick dog' was allegedly said by Thorpe to his then friend Peter Bessell and became the *Daily Mirror*'s front page headline in November 1978.

DOG LEADS TO GOD

of how we treat anyone with less power than ourselves, fellow humans included. Thorpe knew nothing about Rinka until later, but it is unlikely that her death distressed him: inconvenient dogs and awkward humans were to be disposed of as and when a gun became available.

Rinka came back to haunt him. Just two months later, Auberon Waugh made the connection between her death and Thorpe's political ambitions, writing waspishly in Private Eye, 'My only hope is that sorrow over his friend's dog will not cause Mr Thorpe's premature retirement from public life.'[12] In truth it was Scott's intended execution rather than Rinka's actual killing that caused his downfall. Thorpe stood trial in 1979 and although acquitted, he never recovered. Subsequent books, films and podcasts have supported Scott's side of the story.[13]

God watches us. The same God who watches over us also watches how we treat the poorest and the weakest. The Bible frequently states that God is the champion of widows and orphans. And the God who notes even the fall of a sparrow, was surely aware of a young dog so senselessly executed.[14] If we are ever tempted to view others as disposable, we should remember that we all share a common guardian and judge, to whom we are *all* ultimately accountable.

Rinka's story stands as a cautionary tale for politicians, high flyers and everyday people; never kick a pup because the day might come when it will return to bite back, even from beyond the grave.

 Something to chew as your dog walks alongside you
How do I feel about being answerable to God? What kind of God will be asking the questions?

---

[12] Auberon Waugh, *Private Eye* 12 December 1975
[13] *A Very English Scandal*, John Preston Viking Press, 2016
A Very English Scandal, BBC One 2018 miniseries adaptation of the book, by Russell T. Davies and Stephen Frears, starring Hugh Grant as Thorpe and Ben Whishaw as Scott. *British Scandal Podcast*, Season 23: Jeremy Thorpe, January – February 2023, Wondery
[14] Luke 12:6-7

PART 2

LETTING YOUR DOG LEAD YOU THROUGH THE LORD'S PRAYER

4
OUR FATHER IN HEAVEN

I once saw a small dog, looking anxious on the edge of a busy road ... I rushed to help. Things did not proceed as planned.

The road had been built outside the medieval walls of old Toruń to ease the congestion in its narrow streets. I had just finished sketching the city gates when I saw him, small, distracted, jumpy and vulnerable; his golden brown coat would be no protection should he stumble into the fast-flowing river of steel and toughened plastic.

He seemed to be wanting to cross. Foreseeing disaster I blundered in to help. I spoke, trying to draw him to me so I could carry him to safety. He had no wish to let me anywhere near him. I doubt my lack of Polish was the problem. It was more that I was a stranger with an incomprehensible interest in him. No wonder he was afraid. To give myself some credit, I did try to speak gently. I also crouched down and held out a hand, empty (sadly) as I had not packed any dog treats for this trip. I saw that I was making things worse as he backed away from me ... and towards the road. And because he was staring at me, he was ignoring his true danger, the cars. I too backed off. Had he known me, he would have run into my arms but alas I was the wrong person for this dog and for this rescue. Good intentions were clearly not enough.

Later I thought about how God draws close to us. Despite the clichés God seems less interested in showing up in overwhelming, impossible-to-ignore bursts of glory. All those trumpets, angels, clouds and searing rays of dazzling light, so beloved by baroque painters are surely within the repertoire ... somewhere ... but the biblical testimony suggests that they are more the exception than the rule. Perhaps they are all being saved for the grand finale? In the meantime, God usually favours a quieter approach: the unexpected guests,[15] the still small voice,[16] the quiet call in the night,[17] the birth of a tiny baby Jesus in an obscure backwater of the Roman Empire. His career was hardly stellar; a wandering prophet with a degree of local fame who then died a criminal's death ... only to reappear. But even then favouring gently drawing alongside over glorious manifestations.

According to his lesson, 'How best to address God', we should begin directly and personally, 'Our Father in Heaven'. In prayer, it is better to err by being over-familiar than overly respectful: less the terrified grovel and more the, 'Hi, Dad'. I do not know many families who use the formal and starchy sounding 'Father' and if Jesus' original Aramaic word was 'Abba' then 'Daddy' would be a far better translation, encouraging us to believe that God is already closer than we dare to imagine. Despite all God's otherness, power and superiority we can approach with the most intimate trust we know; that of an infant towards a loving parent. This was my mistake in Toruń. I did not earn any trust before launching my rescue attempt and thus put a frightened dog into even greater danger. Mercifully that day there were better forces at work and the dog found its way safely back into the city.

One more thing: 'Our Mother in heaven.' Thoughts? At this juncture, I respectfully disagree with any who insist that because Jesus said, 'Abba' not 'Ima' all discussion about God's gender is permanently closed. God must be more than exclusively male; God

[15] Genesis 18:1-15
[16] 1 Kings 19:11-13
[17] 1 Samuel 3:1-11

OUR FATHER IN HEAVEN

is genderful and certainly not genderless. There are enough biblical images of God as female to convince me that 'Mama' or 'our Ima in heaven' are perfectly acceptable.

We come to God as a human infant comes to a kind mother, the first person they instinctively trust ... and with the same confidence a wolf cub has in their mum.

Something to chew as your dog walks alongside you
Could I ever have the same trust for God as a pup has for its mum?

5
HALLOWED BE YOUR NAME

How long did you spend choosing your dog's name? Did it come in an instant? Or perhaps your dog came already named? The French have a custom of naming dogs according to the year they were born. Apparently this helps vets know how old a dog is. So dogs whose names begin with a 'P' were born in 2019, an 'R' in 2020 and an 'S' in 2021 and so on. This is not enforced as a law but nevertheless its usage is surprisingly common.

The large black mutt we found in the SPA refuge[18] was born in 2019 and had been named 'Pixel', quite incongruously as he bears no resemblance to a tiny computer generated dot. A staff member told us that he did not respond to it and should we wish, we could give him a new name. We spent a fun day swapping suggestions with each other before settling on 'Hugo'; a name which works in both French and English *and* like our own names, begins with an 'H'. It took him a while to get used to it. But at the end of one afternoon's play session my husband commented,

[18] SPA (La Société Protectrice des Animaux) is France's equivalent to the UK's RSPCA and the US's ASPCA, providing care for animals in need.

'Well I imagine everyone in the village knows his name by now.'
'Why do you say that?'
'Erm ... you've been shouting it for the past hour ... rather loudly!'

I wonder what challenges Adam faced in the garden of Eden? According to Genesis, one of his first tasks was to name all the birds and animals.[19] Whether they accepted their new names and how they responded when called, is not recorded. Adam's name-giving duties stopped there. And more significantly, there is absolutely no suggestion that Adam ever invented a name for God or even enquired about it.

According to the biblical narrative, the first recorded curiosity about God's name arose many generations later[20] when Moses, confronted by a burning bush, asked the question and was answered, 'I am who I am'[21]: rendered in Hebrew by the four consonants YHWH and in modern English as Yahweh or Jehovah. God's name came again to prominence soon afterwards when Moses received the Ten Commandments,[22] the third of which warns against its misuse.

Why is this so important? A name after all is just a label to distinguish one thing from another. It does not change a person or an object; as Shakespeare's Juliet so famously maintains, 'a rose by any other name would smell as sweet'. Jesus disagreed. He held God's revealed name to be so important that: one, he never spoke it and two, he instructed us to pray that it be hallowed, or made holy ... which seems strange. How can that which is already too-holy-to-be-spoken be 'made holy'? And how does that sit with Jesus' opening line, inviting all of us, even the muckiest, murkiest and messiest of us, to call God 'Abba'? Is there not a risk that unimaginable purity might be sullied by such familiarity? Any contradictions, however, are found not in God but rather in us, who praise God's name whilst

---

[19] Genesis 2:19-20
[20] The Bible does not have a similarly dramatic revelation story for another name for God, 'Elohim'. It derives from the Canaanite word 'El' meaning God and is possibly a plural.
[21] Exodus 3:14
[22] Exodus 20:1-17

DOG LEADS TO GOD

scorning the needs of our fellow humans and recklessly consuming beyond our need. Somehow in God, familial love and divine holiness are not opposites.

Perhaps God's name is treated as 'hallowed' when spoken with the innate, intimate trust a child has for their parents? Perhaps we are told to pray, 'make your name holy' to remind us of our alarming potential to link it with our less-than-holy agendas? Perhaps those who call ourselves God's people are asking God to repair our human-inflicted damage?

The more I consider this simple phrase, the more mysterious it becomes. One thing I am sure about; God's name cannot be hallowed when yelled in frustration (remember how Hugo's name came to be known in our village?) and even less so when weaponised by one group of humans to humiliate another.

 Something to chew as your dog walks alongside you
Ask yourself: how valuable is my dog's name … and my name … and God's name?

6
YOUR KINGDOM COME, ON EARTH AS IN HEAVEN

But what *is* the Kingdom? When we pray for its coming, what do we mean? What should we expect? Can we imagine a perfect sin-free existence? How can we build the Kingdom when our very efforts to do so undermine it? Our lives are so enmeshed in the harmful systems of this world. Some climate campaigners rely on fossil-fuelled cars to reach their next demonstration. Racial equality activists live in cities that boomed on the back of slavery. Environmentalists buy electric cars whose components' mining and refining causes untold damage. Sports tournaments which foster goodwill between nations are held in countries with dubious human rights records. We have evolved into a world riddled with seemingly intractable contradictions. We compromise. We speak of accepting 'necessary evil'. And dog guardians are by no means immune; we see ourselves as animal lovers but each day we buy dog food which perpetuates the torment of other sentient animals, who are just as clever, playful and sociable as our dogs. On earth, it seems that no righteous path is unstained. But this will not be the case in the age to come … or so we hope.

DOG LEADS TO GOD

When the prophet Isaiah speaks of God's Kingdom, he tackles head-on this issue of animals being slaughtered for food:

> The wolf and the lamb shall feed together, the lion shall eat straw like the ox; ...
> They shall not hurt or destroy, on all my holy mountain, says the Lord.[23]

Former predators present no threat to former prey. How on earth could this ever be? Should we conclude that dogs or at least their lupine ancestors, will become vegans? Will the union of heaven and earth see the rewriting of certain scientific laws, notably those governing diet and digestion? Until that day comes we would no more let wolves into a sheepfold than allow a puppy to play in traffic. This promised Kingdom is clearly beyond anything we are capable of understanding.

Jesus offers some glimpses of the coming reality with parables rooted in everyday life: the Kingdom is like a small seed that becomes a huge tree,[24] like yeast that permeates dough,[25] like a priceless pearl or treasure found in a field[26] and so on. I consider my friends' home to be a parable of the Kingdom. They added Mister B to their family. He was a fourteen-and-a-half-year-old collie, stiff and going blind. Very few people adopt an old dog but they took him in so that his few remaining weeks would be in a home rather than a shelter. Mister B settled quickly, making friends with their other dogs ... even their extremely impertinent Teckel puppy. Five years later, he is still there. He sleeps for most of the day. He does not always make it outside when he needs to go. But he's happy and he will carry on as long as his health permits. A household which welcomes the unwanted and the 'useless' is surely a glimpse of the Kingdom of God, where the poor in spirit belong.[27]

When I become befuddled early into the Lord's Prayer, trying

---

[23] Isaiah 65:25 (see also Isaiah 11:6-9)
[24] Mark 4:30-32, Matthew 13:31-32, Luke 13:18-19
[25] Matthew 13:33, Luke 13:20-21
[26] Matthew 13:44-46
[27] Matthew 5:3

YOUR KINGDOM COME, *ON EARTH AS IN HEAVEN*

to imagine all God's creatures, human, canine, bovine, lupine, vulpine and ovine etc. all living together without fear of exploitation, I remedy this by remembering Mister B dozing safely in the warmth and proceed to pray 'your Kingdom come'.

 Something to chew as your dog walks alongside you
What are my mental images of God's coming Kingdom?

7
YOUR WILL BE DONE, ON EARTH AS IN HEAVEN

Any dog person will have any number of tales about clashes of wills. Your dog will want to:

- sleep with you on your bed and if not allowed, then sleep on your bed while you're out;
- nudge your arm away from your keyboard because, 'how could typing be more important than tummy tickling?';
- eat whatever you're eating;
- eat the wrappers from whatever you've just finished eating;
- follow you into the toilet;
- jump into the car and refuse to get out, saying very clearly, 'We. Want. To. Come. With. You.';
- go outside *again* or come inside *again*, in short be on the other side of any closed door;
- play at bedtime;
- come back only when they've finished sniffing;
- go for a walk ... now!

Sometimes our dogs do not merely wish for these things, their

YOUR WILL BE DONE, *ON EARTH AS IN HEAVEN*

desire becomes overwhelming and all consuming. How often, somewhere on a scale between saddened patience and plain old grumpiness, do we look them in the eye and say, 'Sorry but no – it just ain't gonna happen'? And why? Because we know that if we gave our 'yes' to our dogs' every desire our homes would degenerate into chaos. And worse, our dogs would be unhappy.

I am going to try to shift gears from a dog's will to God's will which is clearly not always done on earth as in heaven; a glance at the headlines on any given day will take you to wars, rumours of wars, nation rising against nation, kingdom against kingdom, earthquakes and famines.[28] That such things are predicted does not make them God's will. But what is 'God's will' and how might we discover it? We all have our own, often highly idiosyncratic hopes as to what God wants and it is all too easy to imagine that anything we want with sufficient fervour *surely* must be God's will too. But on certain divisive issues we cannot *all* be right and so God has to say 'not yet' or just plain 'no' to at least some of us, just as we do to our dogs.

This business of living according to another's will is tricky. We know we cannot submit to our dogs' wills. Humans' wills are contradictory. And God's will is hard to discern amidst our own fears and passionately held beliefs. So how do we discover what God actually wants?

God's will must be a good thing. Jesus thought it should be done. St Paul calls it 'pleasing and perfect'[29]. But it can also be confusing (think of Jesus praying, 'not my will but yours be done' and then being crucified the next day[30]). Maybe God's will needs to be puzzled out at each step? Maybe all we can do is pray, 'your will be done' and trust that God is holding our hand as we proceed, aiming to '… do justice, and to love kindness, and to walk humbly with our God?'[31]

 Something to chew as your dog walks alongside you
If I can see the differences between my plans and my dog's desires, how can I learn the distinctions between my will and God's will and especially when my passions are up?

---

[28] See Mark 13:7-8;   [29] Romans 12:2;   [30] Luke 22:42-43;   [31] Micah 6:8

8
GIVE US TODAY OUR DAILY BREAD

Do you know why our dogs lick our faces? And if they can, our mouths? An adult dog does this as a sign of friendship or of submission, suitable both for humans and for other dogs. So far so good, nothing too alarming here. However when we dig around for the habit's origins, we uncover something truly gross ... or at least gross to humans. Face licking is key to survival. In the wild, wolf pups eagerly await the moment when a parent returns from hunting to feed them. Mum or Dad will arrive with a delicious bag of partly-digested meat; that 'bag' being their belly. How to get meat from Mum to pup? The pup licks her mouth, prompting her to regurgitate the meal. So why do our dogs lick our faces? The polite reply runs; they are re-enacting a vital primal routine. The coarser answer is; they want us to throw up so they can eat the contents of our stomachs. I gave fair warning that this was unpleasant ... but only to us humans. For adult wolves, stomachs offer a simple and efficient way of carrying their puppies' food from the killing site back to the den.

A mother's care does not stop here. She is so determined to keep her pups safe that she removes from the den everything that is highly scented and might attract a predator. Again, lacking plastic bags, she uses her belly; in short, she eats her own puppies' poo. Gross! But only to us humans. We might freak out when our domestic dogs scoff fox poo, 'Why do you do that! It's so disgusting!' But their answer would be, 'This is just another primal and vital routine.'

We are more like wolf pups licking their mother's face and less like shoppers browsing the bakery counter when we pray, 'Give us today our daily bread'. 'Daily bread' means far more than a fresh baguette or bag of sliced loaf; these two words stand for 'everything we need today': food, water, shelter, sanitation … the list goes on.

Do we need to bother making this request? If those of us who live in the West, neglect to ask for Daily Bread, the chances are we will still have food and much more besides. Jesus' original audience probably had a more hand-to-mouth existence and thus took the words more literally. Along with them, we can pray this line with hope and gratitude, reinforcing our complete dependence on God, not just for food but for life itself. Long ago King David offered a gift to God whilst praying: 'all things come from you and of your own have we given you.'[32] In the Lord's Prayer, Jesus is inviting us to make the same acknowledgement and commending an intimate, pup-like trust in God. And how much better to receive with gratitude than simply to take, take and take?

Something to chew as your dog walks alongside you
How often am I aware of how much God provides for me?

And just an extra note, should anyone be offended that I have likened the God who provides to a vomiting she-wolf, I have two things to say. First, wolves are part of God's creation and so the whole licking-vomiting thing is part of God's design. Secondly, is the *way* we humans take food from our surroundings really God's plan? We humans kill 200 million sentient land animals every day (72 billion a year) many knowing nothing but a miserable existence in a factory farm. Anyone wanting to be offended on God's behalf with regard to food should start here.

[32] 1 Chronicles 29:14b

9
FORGIVE US OUR SINS

During chapel services in HMP Manchester, my colleague Jo often used the following absolution;

'God forgives you. Forgive others. *And* forgive yourself.'

Blithely waving aside qualms about liturgical authorisation, she claimed it was simple, direct and free from waffle. She liked its bluntness; it offers no shelter from the challenges of forgiveness whether we are asking for it, offering it or struggling to believe that God has a way forward for us, no matter what we have done.

How might dogs help us to grasp forgiveness? Here is a story about Bella. One day she was off-lead, on a family walk in the countryside. They cut across a field and Bella attacked a sheep. She had never done anything like this before. Her sudden burst of violence came as if from nowhere. All the same, there was no forgiveness for her. She was beaten and banished from the family home. Instead of her soft bed indoors, she slept on concrete outside, chained up in a yard with only a thin coat to protect her during the long winter months. I imagine her utter confusion, her total inability to connect her current state with her previous crime, her sweet nature raising fresh hopes whenever a family member passed by. At some point

FORGIVE US OUR SINS

a male dog must have scaled the wall and she fell pregnant. Her salvation came after her pups had been born and she was taken to be neutered. The appalled vet contacted a rescue group who swiftly intervened and found her a new home. She now sleeps once again on a proper bed ... or on a sofa ... or outside in the sunshine ... or in front of the fire.

Was Bella's crime bad? Yes! Attacking farm animals is one the worst things that a dog can do (or more accurately, that a guardian can allow to happen). Should she have been so punished? Of course not. Should she have been forgiven? In my view, the answer is a resounding YES. It would be unwise to trust her around sheep again but withholding forgiveness was worse than unwise; it was pointless and cruel.

What percentage of dog lovers would side with Bella's former guardians? Hopefully very few, if any at all. But how many whilst advocating forgiveness for Bella, struggle to accept it for themselves? Perhaps the greatest challenge in Jo's absolution is the bit about forgiving ourselves. If this is you, ask yourself two questions:

1. If Bella was my dog, would I forgive her?
   And then,
2. If I could forgive Bella, how much more will God forgive me?

Surely this is all rather simplistic when forgiveness raises so many

complex questions? Maybe. But maybe it is the simplicity of forgiveness that makes it so hard to grasp? We should not allow such exploration to distract us from the central truth: God is a forgiving God. God, in greater love than we can imagine, always desires us to move forward and often provides a way, previously unimagined.

Forgive us our sins.

God forgives you. Forgive others. *And* forgive yourself.

Something to chew as your dog walks alongside you
What obstructs me from receiving forgiveness?

Laika
c.1954 - 3/11/1957

10
AS WE FORGIVE THOSE WHO SIN AGAINST US

If dogs knew how some humans treated them, they might avoid us altogether.

Caution: the following three boxed paragraphs contain descriptions of human cruelty to dogs. If this is not for you today, skip over them.

> In 1911 a Norwegian expedition set out for the South Pole. They left base camp for the final trek with fifty-two dogs. As per their plan, they slaughtered and skinned twenty-four of them en route, to feed the humans and the remaining dogs. Several more died. They returned with only eleven dogs.[33]
>
> In 1954 the Soviets loaded Laika, a stray Moscow

---

[33] *The use and abuse of dogs on Scott's and Amundsen's South Pole expeditions*, Carl Murray, University of Tasmania, January 2008

> mongrel into Sputnik 2 and sent her into space. They made no plan for her return. She died of overheating.
>
> In 2017 UK scientists used 2,496 dogs in 'experimental procedures'.[34] Figures for the US are much higher: PETA puts the annual figure at more than 48,000.[35] Beagles are the preferred breed because they are small and docile.[36]

According to Jesus forgiving others is not an option. It's a command. We are not allowed to love forgiveness for ourselves whilst refusing it for others.[37] Can dogs teach us anything here? They are exceptional forgivers, never returning like for like. If, when lying sprawled across the carpet in the dark we tread on them, they accept it is an accident not an assault. If we forget mealtimes, they patiently remind us. If we stay out too late, they are without judgement just overjoyed to have us back.

Does all this make them experts? Perhaps ... but only to a point. All too often dogs proceed too quickly from forgiveness to a possible second act: 'reconciliation'. Their sense of pack loyalty overrides any fears for their safety, however well-founded. They forgive and renew trust in the same generous breath. Such steadfast loyalty can be pitifully unwise when their guardians are abusive.

There is a long story at the start of the Bible which offers a healthier approach. Young Joseph, naïve, spoilt brash and the apple of Dad's eye is sorely mistreated by his older brothers. His annoying arrogance, however provocative is no justification for their cruelty. Years later, having survived all manner of hardships Joseph meets them all again, only now the tables are turned. He has become an Egyptian overlord, rich with power while they as beggars, have none. He forgives them, in so far as he does not throw them to the crocodiles but he does not trust them ... not immediately. He plays

---

[34] *Animal testing: Which ones are used in UK experiments?* Cherry Wilson, BBC Newsbeat, 4 April 2019
[35] *Dogs in Laboratories*, peta.org
[36] *Why is beagle testing so common?* Naturewatch Foundation, www.naturewatch.org
[37] Matthew 6:14-15

a game with them, falsely accusing Benjamin their youngest brother, of stealing a silver cup. The game could be called, 'What you going to do now when Dad's (new) favourite is in danger?' The brothers rally to Benjamin's side and thus prove that they have changed and are worthy of Joseph's trust. Much weeping ensues and the divided family is reconciled.[38]

Dogs are not so nuanced. They would not bother with silver cups. To them the pack is the pack, no matter how toxic. They conflate forgiveness with reconciliation far too readily and offer their valuable trust without first checking whether it is safe to do so.

I have a hunch that humans all too often, make this same mistake too. We imagine that 'forgiving those who sin against us' means laying ourselves vulnerable to repeated bad behaviour. This path leaves us with two options: receiving further abuse or getting damned for withholding forgiveness. We would save ourselves considerable agonies, if we could disentangle forgiveness from reconciliation, letting the first mean 'relinquishing our right to revenge' and the second, 'an *optional* slow rebuilding of trust'.

Dogs show us the beauty of a forgiving spirit but without the cautions of wisdom. We are commanded to forgive and so forgive we must but after damage has been done, it remains our choice how deeply we are prepared to trust again.

Something to chew as your dog walks alongside you
Is there someone I cannot forgive? Have I ever conflated forgiving with trusting an untrustworthy person?

---

[38] Genesis 37, 39 - 47

11
LEAD US NOT INTO TEMPTATION

Why, on a burning hot July day, am I kneeling on a rough stretch of earth digging yet another in a long line of holes? The ground is hard and full of stones. After a certain depth, tools are of limited use so I'm resorting to my hands. Another fly lands on my neck. As I shift my position, a broken bramble snags my leg. Sweat runs from my dusty brow, stinging my eyes. The blister on my palm breaks and fills with dirt. Why am I doing this? Why?

So many answers but the one I settle on is … love. I am out in 34 degrees of heat because I need to build a fence. It will run alongside a hedge which we once thought was too thick for a dog to penetrate. Once the posts are in, we will break rocks to strengthen their bases before fixing first the tension wires and then the chicken wire. In the two years before Hera arrived Hugo never found any gaps. It took Hera less than two days. (An unkind thought: maybe it was not the hedge, but rather Hugo who was too thick.) She's certainly more inquisitive. I stand up to stretch, back aching and see them both dozing in the shade of a tree. Who's the stupid one here?

But this is what love demands. It requires us to go to extreme

LEAD US NOT INTO TEMPTATION

lengths. Hera senses adventure on the other side of the hedge. I see a road and any number of untested dangers. I can't risk her escaping again. Next time she might get hurt. And the job has to be finished before the dog sitter comes to look after them while we take a couple of days away. So here I am, in a heatwave, digging holes.

We do all sorts of things to protect our loved ones from attractive but damaging things. I have no means of explaining this to my dogs. All I can do, is reduce the possibility of harm. Lead us not into temptation. Because some temptations are too much for us.

The next time I look up from my labours, I see Hera cheerfully scrabbling at an existing stretch of fence, earth flying out behind her as she digs a tunnel. The little sod. But I can't help but love her for her enthusiasm, her innocent expression and her desire to explore. And I take no pleasure in her shock when I yell 'NO!'.

Following any disaster we might look back seeking a 'sliding doors moment', trying to isolate that one small and seemingly innocuous decision after which everything changed. 'If only I'd been wiser ...', 'Why did I ignore that warning sign ...', 'Why was I so impulsive? What happened to my thinking?', 'I regret ever listening to ... ever meeting ...', and so on. Is this a useful exercise? At best, we might learn something helpful. More likely we will find ourselves longing for a time machine, inwardly cursing the immutable laws of physics. At worst, we will approach every new scenario with too much caution, terrified of taking the path to ruin.

Instead we ask God to step in and guide us away from temptation. If we shudder, imagining the various harms that could befall our impulsive dogs, how much more might God wish to block certain paths to us? God holds a far bigger map than ours.

I don't want my dogs to find any exits apart from the proper gate. The siren call of adventure beyond is too tantalising for them. That's why I'm building a whole new fence. And if we go to such lengths to quieten temptation for our dogs, how much more might God do, far beyond our knowing, for us?

Something to chew as your dog walks alongside you

St Paul states that God always protects us from any temptation beyond our power to resist, by providing an alternative path.[39] How has this played out in my experience?

And to what unseen lengths does God go, to protect us from temptation?

---

[39] 1 Corinthians 10:13

12
DELIVER US FROM EVIL (i)

Louis is a fine looking fellow. A Griffon, he stands a tad taller than the average Labrador, his frame slimmer and his hair longer, dark with russet highlights. On the day I met him he was the model of canine dignity: calm, unruffled by the presence of other dogs and keeping close to his guardian. Apparently at home he is quite the puppy; having discovered playfulness only recently, he is doing all he can to catch up.

A year or so before he had been in a pitiful state, newly rescued from the local hunt. Nothing about his life had been healthy: not his diet, his accommodation, his exercise regime nor his interactions with humans. It is not surprising that when he became ill, he lost what little value he had to his owners. He had severe infections in both ears, exacerbated by his damp living conditions. The unremitting pain was so intense, that he was witnessed banging his head on the floor, to knock himself into sleep. Even then he'd often wake himself, screaming.

His rescuers paid for several rounds of surgery followed by course after course of antibiotics until his ears were finally clean. Only then did his coat begin to regrow, some of it had been shaved for his operations but most had simply fallen out, such was his distress.

DOG LEADS TO GOD

His rescuers delivered him from disease, from neglect, from soul-destroying pain and most likely from an early death; in short, they delivered him from evil. It was not cheap and some might question whether so much money should be spent on just one dog. His new guardians have no such qualms as they watch him gambol around, playful and curious, making friends and immersing himself in water at every opportunity (whether convenient or not). The one thing that was beyond repair was his hearing. Louis is now permanently deaf.

Louis did nothing to 'earn' his deliverance. He could not ask and at the time of rescue, his looks were uninviting what with his threadbare coat and his ears oozing with slime that caked both sides of his head. And yet when his rescuers met him, his simple act of being gave him value enough.

When we pray, 'deliver us from evil', we do so to a God who is even more perceptive and more generous than Louis' rescuers. We trust in God's ability to deliver us from evil without and evil within, from threats before us and, as we shall see tomorrow, from threats far beyond our understanding.

One more important lesson from Louis' story; God often works with partners when delivering from evil. We humans are frequently summoned to play a role. It is a great privilege to work in cooperation with God. And surely dogs are invited to add their aid as well.

 Something to chew as your dog walks alongside you
How much does Louis know about his deliverance? How much do we understand about ours?

... AND TO THINK THEY HAVE THE GALL
TO TALK ABOUT US DOGS BEING DANGEROUS!

13
DELIVER US FROM EVIL (ii)

The driver had no idea. He was driving as a driver drives when they forget they share the road with others, presumably relishing his Audi's expensive ability to hug corners at high speeds.

We were walking up a quiet country road, keeping closely to the side as we climbed the high-hedged S-bends back to our home. It was a bright May afternoon and the dogs had enjoyed a good run by the river. Trotting along with us was Nellie, our friends' dog, a bouncy grey and black Setter (well mainly Setter). Her guardians were on holiday and had left her in our care, their anxieties relieved by our daily WhatsApp posts.

We did not hear the car until we saw it. Suddenly it was there.

But this is not a horror story. There was no hideous crash. The Audi did come hurtling down the hill, travelling far too fast. The driver could not have seen more than ten metres ahead of him. Had we still been on the road … who knows what would have been left of us? But three minutes before, we had left the road for a path, a longer but safer route home. The car deftly took the turns. We glimpsed the driver and his passenger chatting happily as they shot down towards the bridge. And then there was just the roar of the engine, echoing across the valley as they climbed the other side.

DOG LEADS TO GOD

We stood in that wake, staring first at each other and then at the dogs who were as clueless as the driver regarding peril so narrowly avoided. One was sniffing the grass. The other was twitching his ears at a rustle in the undergrowth. I found myself wondering what I could have said to Nellie's guardians, assuming that is that I had survived. The driver would have been entirely at fault. But us being in the right, is no replacement for their dog.

Exactly how close had we come to carnage? In this instance we can answer with confidence - three minutes. But what of other occasions? Surely there are many dangers, dodged at the last minute beyond our imagination and about which we remain as oblivious as the dogs that May afternoon? Maybe this is why we pray, 'Deliver us from evil.' And how often does God answer that prayer so successfully that we continue to sniff the grass, blissfully unaware of danger's proximity?

As a guardian, I would not want my dogs to know too much about the Audi or the hundreds of other possible daily threats to their existence. Such knowledge would be too much for them. I consider it enough for them to trust me to look after them, coming to me when I call and staying on the verge until I deem it safe to proceed.

How much more must God want to deliver us not just from danger but also from traumatic hypervigilance? If we fixated on every potential evil, we might never leave home and our lives would never know God's fullness. Bad things will happen to us. Some accidents we will not avoid. Other humans will plan terrors which will damage us and our loved ones. But mercifully these will not come to us every day. We can call our survival chance or good luck, or we could be grateful that God hears our prayer and delivers us from evil in ways far beyond our asking or imagining.

 Something to chew as your dog walks alongside you
If I can do so without falling into hypervigilance, can I count the number of disasters that I have been kept from so far this week?

AHEM! YOU MISSED ONE!

14
FOR THE KINGDOM, THE POWER AND THE GLORY ARE YOURS, FOR EVER AND EVER, AMEN

Love my dogs as I do, sometimes I have a tick-box attitude to them. Walk? Done! Feeding? Done! Training games? Done! Tummy tickle? Done! Good! Now can I get on with my stuff?

Love God as I do, sometimes I discern the same-tick box attitude. Daily prayers? Done! Bible readings? Done! Weekly church? Done! Good! Duty done and now my time is my own.

Neither of these are laudable. Neither God nor dogs should be reduced to a set of tasks … which risks becoming a list of chores.

Of course there will be times when we're feeling stressed and this seems unavoidable. God understands us and our dogs forgive us. But too much of this will shrivel us, precisely by damming two such vital sources of joy.

With God, the theory is all there in the doxology, the ending of the Lord's Prayer, 'For the Kingdom, the power and the glory are yours, for ever and ever, Amen'. Not everyone includes this; many Catholics finish at 'deliver us from evil'. I like it, partly due to familiar habit but mainly for its inescapable reminder that *everything* is ultimately about God. There is no, 'my stuff' or, 'my own time'. Stuff and time are created by God and then loaned to us, to be shared back with God. We do not honour anyone by fulfilling a list of requirements, with an eye on the clock and hearts set on free time. I suspect dogs see through tick-box devotion. And if *they* can then how much more does God?

As for dog theory; we have chosen to open our homes and our lives to a living wonder that cannot be switched on when wanted and off again afterwards. Some people seem to want a dog only for half an hour at the end of each day, for the de-stressing warm welcome home and a spot of canine playtime. They outsource all other dog needs to dog walkers and doggy day care. If this is you, my advice is not to stop having a dog but to re-evaluate your other life choices. No one, on their death bed ever looks back and regrets time 'wasted' playing with a dog.

After theory comes practice: with God, it can take time to build our lives into a prayerful rhythm as we learn what Brother Laurence called 'The Practice of the Presence of God'. With dogs, all we need to do is find a ball and a bit of open space and we're off. When we get both theory and practice right, we benefit; we become more like ourselves.

To observe ourselves engaging in tick-box devotion of any kind is to cross the first hurdle. To God we say, my time is yours, along with the Kingdom, the power and the glory, so help me discover your presence in every moment of my life. To our dogs we might say, your life is short and our days together are precious, so find me your lead and let's take you out.

And if we're really smart we might even find a way of saying both at the same time.

Something to chew as your dog walks alongside you
What is it about being with dogs (and God) *or* being with God (and dogs) that makes me more myself?

PART 3

LETTING YOUR DOG LEAD YOU THROUGH THE CHRISTIAN YEAR

15

ADVENT: THE SECOND COMING

Questions we often ask each other as we near home: 'What have the dogs been up to?' and 'What are we going to find strewn across the floor?' Blessed are those guardians who on returning home, find their dogs alert with tails wagging ... and no part of that home destroyed.

Our dogs can get creative in our absence, using a variety of materials to re-decorate and re-organise. The bin is usually their first port of call but the shoe rack remains a popular second. If truly inspired they'll rearrange the sofa cushions. If we've been careless and left food on the sideboard, we can expect to find containers torn, tooth-pocked and licked clean. If there's a puddle ... well accidents are accidents.

I feel a palpable sense of relief if there is just a single flip flop on the sofa. A fully evacuated recycling bin is another matter. Guardians of puppies face far worse; mercifully both of ours came to us past the chewing phase.

Some of Jesus' parables are popular in Advent, especially those involving a homeowner who returns from an absence of unspecified length and finds everything in order or all in disarray. Either way, servants are called to account; 'Blessed are those slaves whom the master finds alert when he comes.'[40] There are rewards for the watchful and consequences for the inattentive. Christians value such stories when contemplating Jesus' second coming and considering their readiness.

Humans, blessed with far more cranial space for reasoning, have far greater accountability than dogs. There can be no worthwhile upbraiding for dogs after the event, no matter how destructive. Humans have only a two second window in which dogs can associate our rebuke with their action. If we find the wrapper from a block of margarine on the sofa and the cushion strangely greasy, shouting will not discourage repeat performances. The dog might look chastened. Its tail might shoot between its legs as it slinks away, eyes wide in seeming recognition. We might even comment, 'Look at her face, she knows *exactly* what she's done.' But if we do, we are deceiving ourselves. Whenever our dogs look guilty, they are only ever frightened and confused; we have returned home angry and they do not know why. A dog cannot connect a stained sofa cushion with our outrage. There is only one learnable lesson here and it's for us not the dog ... make sure the margarine is safely shut in the fridge before heading out.

Quite what kind of consequences Jesus intends for servants found presiding over disarray remains to be seen: Matthew's account contains some dire warnings,[41] but Luke presents a more encouraging version in which the returning master, finding all well, fastens his belt, sits his servants down and serves them.[42]

If we're good guardians we'll rejoice at our reunions, forgive misdemeanours, not hold our dogs accountable to human standards, mop up messes, re-establish order, take them out for a turn around the block and maybe find them a biscuit.

 Something to chew as your dog walks alongside you
How often do I consider my readiness for a meeting with God? As I anticipate this, am I more joyful or fearful?

---

[40] Luke 12:37a
[41] Matthew 24:45-51, 25:1-13, 25:14-30 see also Mark 13:32-37
[42] Luke 12:35-38

16
ADVENT: JOHN THE BAPTIST

'Very soon, your life will change ... forever!' 'Someone is coming who will make a huge difference to your life ... for the better.'

This might sound like the advent cry of John the Baptist but (far less momentously) it was just little me, trying to explain to one dog (Hugo) that another (Hera) was on her way. I felt he needed some preparation.

We had had him for just over two years. He seemed happy enough but I had often wondered whether something was missing from his life. We had tried to give him all that we humanly could but therein lay the problem. Human love only goes so far. He needed more. He needed contact with his own kind. He needed canine companionship and given his excitable eight-stone size, he was often too much for our friends' dogs.

Then one afternoon the stars and planets all lined up. I was procrastinating, flicking through Facebook when I saw our dog, one I had never met before but without any scintilla of a doubt, *our* dog. A black Labrador cross just like Hugo, who needed a home. She

DOG LEADS TO GOD

was three years old and her name began with an H. 'That's our dog!' Now! How to get her from the screen into our home? *Her* home! Because she clearly belonged here. And how utterly bizarre that she was not already here, by my side.

I launched into an immediate frenzy of phone calls and form filling, the rescue association tempering my enthusiasm with the reminder that this is a long process: if all went well, we might be allowed an initial meeting the following week. They also told me something of her past treatment, a shameful tale of rejection, abuse and neglect (how could anyone do this to any dog, let alone *our* dog!).

The next morning they phoned me with a problem. My heart stopped. But mercifully it was not bad news, quite the opposite; 'Her foster care has fallen through. Can we bring her this evening?' This left me with only a few short hours to prepare Hugo. But how? If the two of them got on then she would stay with us for good. If they did not then we would all miss out on a seismic shift for the better. But how to prepare him to welcome such an unknown quantity? All I could do was repeat, 'Very soon, your life will change ... forever!' 'Someone is coming who will make a huge difference to your life ... so get ready!'

That's about as far as this parallel can be pushed. Even I am blushing slightly as I try to compare our tiny household drama with John the Baptist's mighty task. His call was to prepare the world for someone far, far greater than our beautiful new dog. His audience was more responsive; they came forward for baptism but still they remained rather clueless as to what the coming messiah would be like. John was hardly on the mark himself. He told them to expect someone even more austere, even more alarming than himself: an axe to cut down unfruitful trees, a winnower to clear the threshing-floor, saving grain but burning chaff with 'unquenchable fire.'[43] in short, a description hard to match with the compassionate, persuasive, self-sacrificing prophet from Nazareth.

Maybe I should go no further than noting that John and I agree on the importance of heralding a significant arrival. And in both cases the new arrival brought unimagined joy. For our little family, a

[43] Matthew 3:12 (see also Luke 3:17)

ADVENT: JOHN THE BAPTIST

new dog who turns loneliness into raucous playtimes, for John's far bigger audience, a saviour who turns sorrow into dancing, death into new beginnings and the world upside down (or right way up).

Something to chew as your dog walks alongside you
How would I prepare myself (and others) for such a significant arrival?

17
ADVENT: STAYING AWAKE, KEEPING ALERT

Picture this: a day in grim December. Outside the sky, only half-light at midday, is reflected in the muddy, leaf-choked puddles. Inside it is warm. The dogs, dry at last after their morning walk, are sound asleep on their dog beds which have been moved to their winter positions by the wood burner. All is grey without and at peace within. In the kitchen, I reach for a small cardboard cube, one of twenty-four numbered boxes placed within a handmade wooden frame in the shape of a pine tree, which hangs just above jumping height. In writing this I'm making a confession: I made an advent calendar for my dogs. Two dog treats per box, for each day leading up to Christmas. Soppy? All right, I know, I know! *And* at questionable odds with my usual mantra that dogs are dogs, not little humans.

Today I select box number eleven and ease it out as gently as I can. I do this so well that my human ears detect no sound, before the rustle and crump of beds being abandoned and the skitter of claws across floors. With the box barely an inch from the frame, both dogs are sitting at my feet, eyes fixed on my hand., tails wagging in anticipation. They had learnt this routine by day three.

ADVENT: STAYING AWAKE, KEEPING ALERT

How can dogs go from contented slumber to such alert attention? How can they sleep soundly through howling wind, drumming rain, the clatter of cooking and the chatter of podcasts and yet awaken at the slightest sounds of possible food? And maybe this is how we could be in advent, since we are told to remain awake and to keep watch.

It would be preposterous, dangerous and impossible to take this literally. The world record for staying awake is four hundred and fifty-three hours and forty minutes; just three hours short of nineteen days.[44] But why would anyone, God included, want us to do this? Even after three nights of enforced wakefulness we can start hallucinating. Further out on the extremes sleep deprivation is a form of torture.

So what is the sense behind Jesus' instructions, popular in Advent readings: 'Keep awake ...',[45] 'Beware, keep alert ...',[46] 'Be on guard ... Be alert at all times ...' ?[47] Maybe our dogs have the answer. They have the skill of sleeping whilst remaining attuned to the sounds that matter. They can filter out the widest range of extraneous noises and yet still catch the click of a latch, the fall of footsteps on the path and the faintest whisper of a moving treat bag. During this season our senses are bombarded with cosy festive promises of better Christmases, available for just a bit more cash. Blocking our ears could deaden the din but might we also risk missing the cry of the poor and the voice of God? If only we could somehow learn how our dogs do it.

Something to chew as your dog walks alongside you
How can I learn to ignore the noise whilst staying alert to the sounds that matter?

---

[44] This record is held by Robert McDonald and will not be beaten as in 1997 the Guinness World Records refused to acknowledge further attempts out of concerns for safety.
[45] Matthew 24:42
[46] Mark 13:33
[47] Luke 21:34-36

18
CHRISTMAS EVE

Many people might consider two dogs to be enough. Our friends were comfortably settled with their rescues, George and Choupie when they heard about Malcolm, a fourteen-year old golden Labrador. His guardian had tragically died at the age of fifty-two, entrusting Malcolm to someone who did not have the resources to care for him. Our friends stepped in and offered Malcolm a place in their family. He arrived without ever having to spend a night in a dog refuge. Lucky boy. If only all dogs could be thus treated.

But would there be room for him? The house is large enough but that's not my point. How would the existing dogs take to him? And what about the humans? Would they have room in their hearts for yet another, especially one who might soon leave, given that his days were drawing to their natural end? The answer was an unequivocal 'yes'. Canine hearts are vast and human hearts have more elasticity than we might credit. Malcolm was welcomed by all. Initially he suffered from separation anxiety and so he accompanied his humans whenever they went out. He might have been a bit confused but mercifully he will never guess at the desolation that drew so near to him.

The author Ellis Peters peppers her Brother Cadfael mysteries with wonderful asides. One such is an observation about the range of the human heart which she calls 'terrifyingly wide'.[48] Our scope for goodness *and* for meanness is difficult to take in and at times, deeply worrying.

We need to be realistic; sometimes tragedies come when pet lovers cannot say 'no' and the RSPCA gets called to a house filled with more dogs than can be loved, exercised and fed. God has no such limits. There is always room for one more in God's heart.

Jesus speaks of God's heavenly home having plenty of room,[49] which on Christmas Eve leads us to remember an expectant couple far from home, hoping that someone somewhere in Bethlehem will find a space for them. We can overdramatise this story by adding little donkeys, cold-hearted innkeepers and Mary teaching Joseph how to be a midwife. The truth is, there was 'no room' because every household's guest room[50] was already packed with other family members also summoned for the Roman census, leaving no suitable space for a woman to give birth. But 'no room' was not the end of it. Where room could not be found, room was made. It took a bit of imagination but that's humanity: our scope is wide. We can be generous, creative and accommodating. We can also be downright vile. Herod denied any room in his realm for a potential rival and slaughtered every boy under the age of two in Bethlehem. Our scope, as humans is indeed terrifyingly wide.

And at Christmas, Christians celebrate the mystery of God becoming one of us, entering our 'terrifyingly wide' condition as a helpless new-born baby. Whether we have room for this baby and the person he grew to be, is up to us. Making such room will bring changes and certain restrictions, but mostly liberations. God nurtures our hearts, enabling us to find room for the lost ... even for an old dog.

Something to chew as your dog walks alongside you
When has love challenged my limits and enabled me to find (or make) a bit more room?

---

[48] *The Holy Thief*, Ellis Peters, Headline 1992
[49] John 14:2
[50] The confusion arises because 'kataluma', the Greek word for 'guest room' is also the same as the word of 'inn'

19
CHRISTMAS DAY[51]

Me, seven years old, on Christmas morning arguing with my Mum about feeding the dog extra treats …

Me: 'But why not? It's Christmas Day.'
Mum: 'Because he's a dog. He doesn't understand. For him it's just another day.'
Me: 'But it's Christmas Day!'
Mum: 'Not for him. If we spoil him today, he'll expect the same every day after this. It will confuse him'
Me: 'But it's Christmas Day!'

She won in the end and clearly her words sank in since I can still remember them all these years later. In our end of term school assembly, we had been told a story about the night Jesus was born and how the animals in the stable were given the power of speech. Being fanciful, I wanted this to be true but Mum's logic brought me back to earth. She was right. Christmas is a human festival and it is not fair to allow it to disrupt our dogs' routines too much.

[51] For dog-related musings on the incarnation, please see chapter 2, If I could talk to the animals… in *The Dog Walker's Guide to God* (2023)

CHRISTMAS DAY

Many would disagree. During the cost of living crisis, many struggling for spare money skimped on their office's Secret Santas rather than deny their dogs. In 2022 Brits spent between an estimated £873 million[52] and £1.3 billion[53] on Christmas presents for their pets.

St Paul might also disagree, despite him not being a renowned animal advocate. He writes about God's salvation as a gift for more than humans alone. There is a glory to come that will be for *all* creation. Current laws about ageing and dying, our 'enslavement to decay' will be no more. This prompts, even now, a *creation-wide* collective longing, a groaning in anticipation for God's promised freedom.[54] If Paul is right, this is good news not just for humans but also for every other living thing, including dogs. What will this look like in practise? Is it the same as Isaiah's version of a Kingdom where wolves live peaceably alongside lambs?[55] If it is hard to envisage the final outcome of God's plan, its beginning could not be more familiar … a woman gives birth to a child. St John skips all the details about Bethlehem, shepherds, stars, seers and slaughter and instead offers a summary; 'God so loved *the world*' …' not 'God so loved human beings' … that he gave his only Son.[56] Christmas cannot be restricted to humans alone.

All the same, Mum made an undeniable point. Our dogs need their routines. Consistency is important and too much deviation is bound to cause confusion. Dogs do not share our capacity to rationalise Boxing Day blues. Also Mum had an aversion to the word 'spoil' which is all too carelessly brandished around at Christmas ('We really spoilt the grandchildren this year', 'She's been having a hard time, so I decided to spoil her rotten with loads of extra presents'). 'Spoil' is a poor swap for 'treat'. Try saying those same

---

[52] *Christmas: It's a furry affair*, www.co-operative.coop/media/news-releases, 21 December 2022
[53] *Dog owners set to spend 10% more on Christmas gifts this year*, guidedogs.org 17 November 2022
[54] Romans 8:18-23
[55] Isaiah 11:6-9, 65:25 (more on this in the Lord's Prayer section – 6. Your Kingdom come)
[56] John 3:16

sentences but substituting spoil's synonyms: impair, ruin, trash, tarnish, damage, wreck and so on. You would not want to do any of these to a loved one, human or canine.

The original Christmas story has nothing to do with sentimentality or self-indulgence and certainly not spoiling but rather love that has gone to extraordinary lengths, in great humility to meet us in our deepest needs and bring to us, in the most unexpected yet entirely relatable form (a tiny baby), the presence of God.

 Something to chew as your dog walks alongside you
What does my dog need most at Christmas? What do I need most at Christmas?

OH MY! TWO OF THESE GIFTS SMELL INTRIGUING!

20
EPIPHANY (THE FEAST)

The wonders of the internet! What did I type into a search engine to elicit the following list?

★ A portable mini vacuum cleaner (for hair) ★ a USB chargeable paw washer, ★ a backpack (100% breathable) with a head hole ★ a fully transparent plastic raincoat ★ a super-absorbent floor pad for pee & poo ★ a rainproof leash with built in mini-umbrella ★ a pet selfie stick ★ a bone shaped necklace & tag (in two pieces) ★ a safety gate ★ various toys and T-shirts.

The answer? 'best gifts for a new puppy?' With the exceptions of the safety gate and the absorbent pad, they are gloriously frivolous and entirely designed to please humans, not dogs. Further searching ('most expensive gift for a dog?') revealed a dog dress costing £40,000 and containing 40,000 hand-applied crystals (a process which took nine hundred hours). My scorn is slightly tempered by my earlier confession about my dogs' wooden advent calendar and the fact that whenever a friend gets a new dog, I visit with a gift, usually a cheap toy not a tiny diamond studded tiara.

What is the best gift for a new baby? Gold, frankincense and myrrh might at first look like equivalents of a $31,660 'Hello Kitty' dog bed as a gift for a pup.[57] What is a small child going to do with them? To be fair, we are not told how much gold the Magi brought to Jesus and a bit of extra cash is always handy. Frankincense less so. As for myrrh ... if its prime use is anointing a dead body, well it's simply bad taste. Along with the bizarre nature of the gifts, we have the intriguing story of the givers and their journey. Astrologers operating far from the Holy Land and God's revealed Law, see a new star rising in the heavens. Their skills reveal that it heralds the birth of a new king and without further ado, they set forth to pay homage. The star, like early sat-navs, gets them almost to their destination but not quite, rather they end up in nearby Jerusalem where they dent any claim to being 'wise' by blabbing the news to a murderous old tyrant that he has a new-born rival.

There are rules to gift-giving, involving concealment and disclosure. We begin with discrete planning and secret procurement. Wrapping and other forms of hiding come next. At the moment of revelation, there are at least two responses: a 'ta-dah' unveiling, accompanied by complete overwhelming ('Oh Daddy! A Porsche!') versus a quieter initial underwhelming ('That's ... erm ... lovely. How thoughtful. What is it?') Gold might have belonged to the first but frankincense and myrrh only revealed their relevance later. Really well chosen gifts continue to deliver, as unravelling mysteries whose significance increases with time.

Those who consider Jesus of Nazareth to be God's greatest gift to the world, recognise these dual themes of concealment and revelation; his birth in obscure Bethlehem is followed by a stream of epiphanies (or moments of great and sudden realisation). With our dogs and our friends' dogs, we might copy the Magi and begin with gifts. After a while, as we discover the outpouring of unconditional love, we realise that we will always be more recipient than donor.

Don't miss the cautionary note in Matthew's story, about how easy it is to avoid an epiphany. The scholars in Jerusalem could have visited the Christ-child: Bethlehem lying just a short hop from the city centre. When Herod called them all together, he asked where the Messiah would be born. They answered, quoting the appropriate

[57] I wish I was kidding but someone has made one of these.

EPIPHANY (THE FEAST)

scriptures, 'In Bethlehem of Judea'.[58] But despite knowing this ... and having a far shorter journey than the Magi, there is no record of any of them bothering. 'The world is full of magic things, patiently waiting for our senses to grow sharper.'[59] The same could be said for God ... and for our dogs but without some effort and observation from us, we will surely miss out.

 Something to chew as your dog walks alongside you
What is my greatest hindrance to discovering new things ... about my dog, about the world, about myself ... and about God?

---

[58] Matthew 2:5-6
[59] W. B. Yeats

21
EPIPHANY (THE SEASON)

'Just how stupid are you?' is not a question I'm ever going to warm to, even when deserved. It was fired at me, as I explained how Hugo when newly adopted had run away from us, straight towards some other dogs and walkers, causing a degree of panic and chaos.

'But how did he get loose from you? Did he somehow slip his lead?'

'No ...' I answered, guessing and not liking where the conversation was going.

'So what happened?'

I continued rather weakly, 'Erm ... I was trying to walk him off-lead ...' before explaining, 'I did this with my previous dog; one full month on the lead at all times before letting him have a bit of a run around by himself.'

'So! It worked for one dog and you just assumed it'd be exactly the same for another dog ... a completely different dog, with a completely different personality and a completely different history?' And before I could nod, the question had been fired, 'Just how stupid are you?'

Leaving all debate about my own follies on one side, the key point is that we must not come to a new dog with too many

EPIPHANY (THE SEASON)

assumptions, regardless of however much experience we think we already have. No two dogs are the same. We need to get to know each one, spending time discovering their likes, dislikes, talents, quirks, fears and oddities.

Epiphany is the season when Jesus 'comes out'; through a set of stories, the world gets to see who he really is. John, after some initial reluctance, baptises Jesus and then depending on the liturgical year, Jesus reveals his identity by: changing water into wine, calling his disciples, healing the incurable and explaining how God's Kingdom surpasses any previous imagining. We find many people feeling confounded; some none too happy about it. 'You're totally off the mark, there's no way you're from God!' (my paraphrase of their collected complaints.)

Jesus challenges some deeply engrained opinions about God's likes and dislikes. He causes outrage in his hometown of Nazareth. He claims to tick the prophet Isaiah's boxes for the coming messiah; anointed by the Spirit to proclaim God's favour ☑ good news to the poor ☑ sight for the blind ☑ freedom for the oppressed and imprisoned ☑ But then he stops, cutting Isaiah's check-list short. He ends the reading mid-passage, rolls up the scroll and hands it back to the attendant, emphatically editing out the bit about proclaiming God's vengeance.[60] Things head downhill after this, resulting in a botched attempt on his life. The season of Epiphany, done properly, is not the cosy confirmation of everything we already know about God but rather its disruption.

But what about those of us who have been church-going for ages? Do we really need to repeat this process every year? Jesus is still the same Jesus as he was last year and will be the same again next January; yesterday, today and forever the same!'[61] True enough but we change. Our teenage selves might be all but unrecognisable if placed alongside our middle-aged or retired versions. Life's great events shape us: finding love ... or not, gaining and losing employment, becoming parents ... or not, encountering grief and deteriorating health. A lot can happen to us between the ages of fifteen and forty-five ... and sixty-five and so on. How could we

[60] Compare Luke 4:14-30 and Isaiah 61:1-2
[61] Hebrews 13:8

DOG LEADS TO GOD

imagine our beliefs would remain unaffected? If we think Jesus is going to look exactly the same to us now as he did even five years ago, the question may well come and bite us, 'Just how stupid are you?' Because we are constantly changing, each season of Epiphany should bring us different angles, new joys and fresh disruptions: a process, not dissimilar from learning to live with an unknown dog, at least in essence if not in magnitude.

Something to chew as your dog walks alongside you
When did I last find a long-held belief about God challenged and confounded?

WHICH OF THESE TWO CATEGORIES IS INCORRECT?

22
LENT

Do you have *that* friend whose dogs are simply in another league when it comes to obedience? Where your beloved pooch may *or may not* respond to you (even though you have treats and your repeated calls are growing increasingly frantic) your friend needs but to murmur a command and her dogs skid to a halt, whatever they are doing, no matter how intriguing the smells involved. We have such a friend. She speaks and her two German shepherds trot cheerfully to her side. They are so beautifully behaved that I can barely stand it. They do not need leads when out in the countryside because they stay close at all times. If they spot a distant hare, lolloping across the horizon, just one word gently but firmly spoken, dissuades them from launching off in pursuit.

I was very surprised therefore when my friend told me that one of them, the younger, needed to return to basic training. For some reason she had lost a bit of her steadiness. Maybe she was developing an anxiety. Maybe something had confused her. The upshot was a change in her behaviour. The remedy was simple; back to basics. The lead came back for all walks and the simple ground rules were revisited until steadiness was re-established. My friend explained that all dogs need this from time to time. When something goes awry, revisiting the basics is often the fix.

Christians frequently go awry. Some days the blessed intentions of our early morning devotions can vanish as quickly as the dew; we can be unexpectedly thrown by a cruelly worded text, an invitation to gossip or a burst of frustration with someone (who ought to know better!). Sometimes persistent issues mount up and if we stop to examine ourselves, we find that we are no longer moving Godwards but backwards.

Lent is a good time for such a stop: an annual check-up, an MOT for the soul. If we use Lent wisely, it is not a prompt for another diet and certainly not an excuse for some macho challenge in self-denying abstinence. There is a story about how St Francis once went to a small, lonely island on Ash Wednesday and gave strict instructions not to be disturbed until Maundy Thursday. There were no houses or even shelters and no food apart from the two loaves he took with him. On collection, he was found to be in excellent spirits, claiming to have fasted for the entire time, consuming no water and just half a loaf which he had eaten only so that his followers would not imagine that his discipline rivalled Christ's forty days in the wilderness. I have a lot of questions. Did he really do this? Did God tell him to? What was the fruit of such a feat? Did he grow in kindness, faithfulness and love? How did he manage to go for so long without water (because humans simply cannot)? And what kind of God gives this kind of instruction and why?

I would not recommend such a test of endurance to anyone. Instead I applaud my friend and her younger dog. They underwent a mini Lent. They stepped back. They made an assessment, found something needed to be corrected, returned to basics and made the required changes.

For Christians the basics are prayer, fasting and alms giving. Lent is a good time to review all three. It might be, owing to the busyness of our lives, that we need to create some space to do this properly so maybe we will decide to give up something; whatever the human equivalent is of temporarily losing off-lead walks. Ideally during Easter we should be able to look back, treasuring the extra time spent with God and joyfully aware of hope renewed and a degree of steadiness restored.

LENT

 Something to chew as your dog walks alongside you
How quickly do I notice when I'm losing my steadiness? What do I do about it? How might God help me?

23
MAUNDY THURSDAY

Food is important for dogs. Very important. I know only one dog with a 'take it or leave it' attitude to food. All other dogs are fully signed up to team 'take it'. Food is fuel. Over the course of sixty million or so years, carnivorans evolved as caniformia, then canids and then wolves, refuelling themselves less with regular meals and more by feast or famine. During the last few thousand years,[62] dogs have not forgotten this. For them, food is not to be gently savoured around a shared table but rather bolted down in large quantities as who knows when the next opportunity will come. Some mealtimes can be explosive, if one dog fears their intake is being eyed too closely by another. There is fellowship but only before the meal. Hunting must be a social activity. Wolves and dogs rely solely on their teeth, unlike felines their non-retractable claws cannot grip and rip. A lone wolf has no chance of bringing down an elk unaided, so the pack works together. They identify the weakest in a herd, isolate it, injure its shoulders and flanks until, finally exhausted it collapses and its body is wolfed down.

---

[62] Between 12,000 and 33,000 years ago; there are a wide range of opinions on this.

MAUNDY THURSDAY

Food is important to humans too but for different reasons. We have significantly upped the game from mere lupine refuelling. Cramming down as much food, as quickly as possible is frowned upon. Also 'food-guarding' is rare among humans, on the contrary we often seek the company of others. As we eat together, we relish flavours both familiar and new, as we talk and talk and talk. The sharing of food is often secondary to the sharing of news. Different cultures have developed fascinating rituals around table fellowship. In Japan, a simple cuppa with the neighbours has evolved into an elaborate ceremony. In France, workers are forbidden from eating lunch at their office desks, not just by convention but by law.[63] How were things in the Holy Land two thousand years ago? We cannot know every detail but we can make a list of Jesus' significant conversations and see how many involved food.

Given humans' and dogs' diverging approaches around food, disaster looms whenever we play self-indulgent games, forgetting that dogs are dogs and inviting them to share our meals. Dogs are happier without confusion. Their food should always be given to them separately. This can be directly by human hand[64] or placed in their bowls or hidden outside for them to sniff out.[65] There are plenty of ways for us to show our dogs affection but bringing them to our tables is not one such. The gulf in understanding is too wide.

If there's a step change, incomprehensible to dogs, in the way humans understand food, is there an even higher step change, similarly lost on us humans, as we approach God's table? What is God's take on food? Being human, I have no definitive answer. However the Bible offers some clues: God uses a prepared table to elevate his loved ones in the sight of their enemies,[66] God is planning an extraordinary feast for all nations, at which sins will be forgiven, death will be abolished and all tears wiped away[67] and most

---

[63] French Law: Code du travail - Article R4228-19 (dating from 1894) This was suspended during the pandemic but only temporarily.

[64] Hand feeding is a wonderful (if messy) way to help an anxious dog learn to trust their human.

[65] Even a semblance of scavenging for food counts as 'wolf work', see Chapter

[66] Psalm 23:5

[67] Isaiah 25:6-8

DOG LEADS TO GOD

incredibly Jesus institutes a new type of meal for his followers.[68] On a Thursday night, his last before he died, he ate with his disciples. Towards the end of the meal he broke open a loaf of bread and gave them all a piece. Then using just one cup, he gave them each a sip of wine. This new 'meal' is no great shakes, at least in canine terms of refuelling. But this is God's table, not theirs or ours. Two millennia later, Christians are still enraptured by Jesus' words. How can broken bread be his body? And the wine? Surely we should be wary of overfamiliarity; surely the offer of a drink of blood should cause a moment of consternation?

These 'glimpses' entice us. They suggest that God's understanding of food is on yet another level. Who can predict what will happen should we open the door to God's knocking and, in God's words, 'I will come in to you and eat with you, and you with me.'[69] It is certainly foolish for us to share our own tables with our dogs but what risks, mysteries and possible confusions lie in store for us when seated at table with God? Even so, that is the invitation we humans have been given.

Something to chew as your dog walks alongside you
What meaning do I attach to Holy Communion? How important is this, compared with other ways of meeting with God?

---

[68] Mark 14:21-23, Matthew 26:25-27, Luke 22:18-20
[69] Revelation 3:20

WARNING!
THIS IS A DIFFICULT READ CONTAINING
DESCRIPTIONS OF BRUTAL CRUELTY.

24
GOOD FRIDAY

> **Warning: this is a difficult read containing descriptions of brutal cruelty.**

Facebook monitors where I linger and then delivers similar posts, resulting in a constant stream of dog-related video clips. These come in three categories, first - the cute: dogs diving into piles of newly raked leaves, puppies snuggling together in front of a warm fire and so on. Then come the more challenging reels, beginning with a filthy diseased mutt living on the streets but always ending well. Once such dogs have been: lured into a cage, driven to a shelter, fed, washed, treated and healed, their fur regrows resulting in a heart-warming final shot of them bouncing around in a loving home. The final type of video is simply horrific; lorry loads of dogs being driven to meat markets where they will be slaughtered and their bodies butchered for human consumption. The live dogs are often in bags, tied at the neck or around the muzzle, leaving either their whole terrified heads or just their noses sticking out. In one haunting shot the rescuers' camera goes inside a sack to reveal a dog, collapsed in panic, wide eyed and panting frantically. She has reached the point of utter helplessness. She has no power, no agency to prevent the coming brutality, the violent theft of her life.

With a couple of clicks I could block this third category of clips from ever reappearing on my screen, sealing forever my cosy bubble from the cries of the afflicted. Thus far I have not. It seems cowardly. Some days, however, they are too much and I scroll over them, hating their pain, my impotence and my complicity (by dint of being human like the perpetrators). Humans are unique in Creation; we are the only species to have mechanised protracted cruelty against our fellow animals ... and all for that most temporary of gains, the pleasure of a meal. And we do so in ways that are all too easy to ignore; there are reasons why abattoirs don't have glass walls.[70]

On Good Friday, I recount the horror of the dog meat trade **not** as an equivalence for, but rather as a window onto the suffering of Jesus. We risk being anesthetised to the cruelty of his crucifixion by the triple threat of familiarity, theologising and the gentleness of western art; too many have painted a nicely toned Jesus, doe-eyed and peacefully resigned to his fate, all distress delegated to the female onlookers. One might surmise a sighing whimper rather than his final cry of desolation. Roman cruelty was truly agonising. As for the theologising; a short story. A school teacher once proposed that a time machine's greatest purpose would be rescuing Christ from the cross. As a newly-converted and fully-fired-up seventeen-year-old, I was appalled; this 'rescue' would deprive us of our eternal salvation. I had some theological ground beneath my feet but I had moved far too quickly to personal gain, aided by over-familiar aphorisms as I scrolled past Christ's pain. His suffering was beyond awful. We will never plumb its mysterious depths but maybe, a snapshot of innocent dogs bound for slaughter, might offer a new perspective into the agonies of this innocent man.

Where to go from here? Are we doomed to finish this reading on such a helpless note? Maybe we should since Good Friday first time around ended without hope. Jesus' disciples went to bed seemingly insensible to his promises of resurrection. Nowadays we know that joy is coming and we barely have time to prepare.

[70] The original quotation runs, 'If slaughterhouses had glass walls, everyone would be vegetarian' - Paul McCartney

GOOD FRIDAY

We crunch gears as we arrange flowers, redecorate churches and rehearse Easter hymns. Back then, on the actual Good Friday, such thoughts were anathema.

There is no consolation for dogs facing slaughter. Their agonies continue. South Korea is hoping to end the industry, maybe in 2027. Other dog-eating countries still lag behind. Even in South Korea the ban is controversial with many older people reluctant to surrender their treasured belief that eating dog flesh helps combat the heat of high summer.[71] If we want to find hope here, the onus is on us to protest whilst supporting dog rescue charities in South East Asia.[72] And if the horror of dog-eating in other countries aids our contemplation of Christ's sufferings, we might also allow it to question our own habits in which other animals, different to dogs (but equally sensitive and equally terrified) are slaughtered for our own tables.

 Something to chew as your dog walks alongside you
Is it possible to have a world free from cruelty? And even if not, what can I do to reduce my complicity in the suffering of others?

---

[71] *South Korean Farmers Threaten to Release 2 Million Dogs in Protest of Dog Meat Ban*, Koh Ewe, TIME 30/11/2023

[72] If interested you could consider supporting an agency such as the Soi Dog Foundation (www.soidog.org).

25
EASTER SUNDAY

Sophie is a two-year-old, doe eyed beagle. When we met her she seemed a calm soul (at least until some food appeared). She was evidently loved by a family once upon a time but then ... they dumped her. Who knows why? Perhaps it was because an ear infection had rendered her deaf and they did not want a disabled dog. They had never had her chipped and so they could not be traced. Had she been merely lost, they could have visited the local shelter or searched for her on petalertfrance.com. They did neither and instead our friends adopted her. The problem is Sophie cannot believe that she will not be abandoned again. She becomes extremely agitated whenever they go out, even if only for a short while. She is being trained how to cope. They have gentle exercises such as leaving her alone in a room initially only for a minute or so before returning, and then gradually increasing their length of absence. It is slow work, always building on yesterday's achievements and not fretting when her anxieties become overwhelming.

Sophie's condition is unusual only in the matter of degree since all dogs experience separation anxiety to some extent. Most merely go quiet when they realise we are going out but it is clear that they don't like being left. Each parting contains the seeds of tragedy. We

EASTER SUNDAY

can offer all the reassurances we like but somehow they never truly believe us.

The flipside is their joy at our return, 'What's all this fuss about? We told you we would be back?' we say as they mob us. Most dogs give an extravagant welcome-home even when we have just popped to the shops. But if we've been out for a whole evening, you might imagine that we were missing, presumed dead and the planning of our funerals is now being disrupted by our sudden reappearance, such is their joy.

Jesus' chosen twelve had been told, on at least three occasions that he would be back ... after dying *and* rising again. Somehow this had not sunk in. Maybe they had not listened at all. Maybe it had been in one ear and out of the other. Maybe their fears had grown like weeds, choking all memory of his words, so that by the second morning they were so deep in separation-despair that not even the women could shake them. 'We have seen him!' they said. 'What an idle tale!' they replied.[73] It took a whole week before all the remaining eleven apostles (Thomas being the late adopter) allowed joy to replace anguish.

Easter joy rises above all else, stronger than our most tenacious fears, more consoling than our deepest woes, more powerful than death itself. It is a powerful driver of healthy Christian growth. Jesus is risen. He left us indeed but then he returned. And now we can never be so abandoned again.

For Sophie and for all our dogs, our every return home contains a spark of Easter joy, bursting into flame within them as they welcome us. Their chorus of, 'They're back!' is in distant harmony with the women's, 'He is risen.' Of course, Easter joy is far greater but maybe our dogs' joyful reaction to us can kindle our response to Jesus on Easter Sunday *and* throughout the year. Hallelujah, he's back! It's him! We've not been forsaken. We are not alone! He's back indeed, hallelujah!

 Something to chew as your dog walks alongside you
What else can my dog teach me about joy?

---

[73] Luke 24:11

26
ASCENSION

'You're far too attached to that dog.'

I usually shrug and smile whenever one of my peers criticises me like this. They also mutter that my dogs are 'child substitutes' like this is a bad thing. If this is a crime, I stand guilty as charged. I have strong parental instincts but no children. My dogs meet many of those needs. And this only becomes a problem, if I ever forget that dogs are dogs, not small humans.

It is not just us never-parents who do this. I have dog-devoted friends whose children have flown the nest. And other friends who have small children *and* dogs at the same time. I suspect that when 'child substitute' is an accusation, what they really mean is, 'you're being very foolish to invest so much in your dog'.

Non-dog people struggle to understand why we, the dog-loving, are happy to:

- never stay out too late,
- walk in the rain,
- pick up poo,
- put up fences around a garden,
- live with dog hair everywhere,

ASCENSION

- limit the kind of holidays we choose (dog friendly accommodation only, near dog friendly beaches)
- demand daily photos and videos from the sitter, should we be parted from our dogs,
- and generally make so much fuss about a being who has a relatively short life.

Those of us who are dog people find none of these onerous. Any negatives are so comprehensively compensated by the joys that abound in a dog-loving home.

Of course God has no equivalent peers but just for a moment, let's suspend the usual theological cautions and imagine that such beings existed. I picture them taking God to one side and having a quiet word about 'this obsession you have with humans'.

'You know they're really not worth it. They are weak willed, they can be treacherous and their lives are less than a blink of an eye. Don't you think that maybe just maybe you've gotten yourself a bit over attached?'

If the Christian doctrine of the incarnation is correct then the word 'attached' is not enough. God so loved the world, that God's own son, God's very self was born of a woman thus becoming one with humanity. It is a phenomenal claim and only grows in its daring as it continues to its logical conclusion as Jesus rises from the tomb and then ascends into heaven. He does not shed his nail-pierced body on the way up but quite what happens to his humanity after this point is a mystery beyond me.

It is outrageously audacious to even consider these matters. Are we really to imagine that the God who created more than the observable universe (which has a diameter of roughly 28.5 gigaparsecs or 93 billion light-years or 8.8×1026 m *and* is billions of years old) would go to such lengths out of love for us short-living humans who exist on only one small planet? If so then God's peer group (even though they don't exist) might have more than a few things to say, 'You've done what!' and 'Isn't it beyond foolishness to invest so much in these beings?'

This is so much more than us getting a tattoo of our dog's face and name. God's attention to us is even more mind-boggling than

DOG LEADS TO GOD

trying to fathom the dynamics of resurrection and ascension. But we humans are granted a glimpse of such all-consuming love when we are privileged to become parents, or merely experience parental love for another being, even a dog. An onlooker might brand it as foolishness and maybe they have a point but those who experience this love know that it is worthwhile beyond all doubt.

Something to chew as your dog walks alongside you
Is my love for my dog foolish? And if so, how foolish is God's love for me?

27
PENTECOST

Martin Laird writes about meeting a man walking with his four dogs, all Kerry Blue Terriers.[74] The dogs were enjoying their freedom, charging around, chasing each other and making the most of a generous open space. But not all four; one dog stayed close to his master, running just a short distance ahead before returning.

One day Martin asked the man why this one dog did not run out with the other three. He explained, this fourth dog grew up in a cage. Small circles were his entire world for so long that now he could not imagine anything else. Not the wide-open landscape nor the examples of the other three, could dissuade him from sticking to what he knew.

Martin then turns to his reader, saying that our human thoughts can be similarly restricted. We have all creation to explore with our minds but all too often we limit ourselves, sticking with the familiar, chuntering round and around on the same tracks.

I don't know what healing there might be for the fourth dog but for us humans, I value the story of Pentecost, God's long-promised, heart and mind-expanding intervention. God's Holy Spirit is poured out

---

[74] *Into the Silent Land: The Practice of Contemplation*, Martin Laird, Darton, Longman and Todd 2006

upon the followers of Jesus, liberating them to imagine new possibilities. Immediately prior to Pentecost, they had lived in hiding, so constricted by fear that they did nothing with the incredible story of Jesus' resurrection. They had seen him die and be buried and yet soon after they had met him, spoken with him, eaten with him and even touched him. But what next? They could not conceive of all this could mean, so they sat and waited, talking round and around in the same small circles.

How can we begin to imagine what lies beyond our usual mental routine? How can we guess at what more God might be offering when we do not know what we do not know? Maybe the key is embracing 'not knowing', literally welcoming 'agnosticism'. I know it might sound perverse to propose agnosticism as part of God's gift at Pentecost but I am talking less about uncertainty as to the deity's existence and more about a mindset that acknowledges the very tiny bite our brains take from the huge cherry of all there is to know ('a-', meaning without and 'gnosis' meaning knowledge). Admitting our 'not knowing' is liberating. Someone seeking to *master* all knowledge will become crushed at discovering all there is yet to learn. The agnostic (in this most literal sense) by contrast, stands on the doorstep of undiscovered countries, never wishing to conquer but delighted to explore. One of my favourite sayings is, 'The greatest enemy of learning is knowing.'[75] If we are convinced that we are expert drivers then our road skills are unlikely to improve. If we think we have faith and God sorted, then our spiritual growth is on hold and like the poor Kerry Blue Terrier, we are doomed to continue running in our little circles.

I do not know if that fourth Kerry Blue ever broke free. I hope so. I don't believe that God wishes any of us, human or canine to remain permanently limited by a harsh past. God's gift of Godself at Pentecost opens to us the wider field.

> **Something to chew as your dog walks alongside you**
> How would I know if my thoughts only ran in limited circles? And if I discovered this to be the case, what could I do about it? How might God help me?

[75] Attributed to John C. Maxwell

28
ORDINARY TIME

Why does such a large chunk of the Christian year get lumbered with such a dull title? Ordinary! Ordinary? Who wants ordinary, whose synonyms are: commonplace, routine, mundane and dull? Why not stick with the magical heights of Christmas, the challenges of Lent, the rollercoaster of Holy Week and Easter and the dizzying possibilities of Pentecost?

I changed my thinking on this one afternoon in my previous job, as a prison chaplain. I had taken a young man to the chapel for some quiet. His grandmother had died and he was not permitted to attend her funeral, so I offered the best I could in the circumstances; some time off the wing, the chance to light a candle and if he wanted, to say some prayers. I made a brew and we sat in the stillness, in the one place in the prison with no visible bars on the windows. After a while he told me about his life, a tale of disorder and instability: a mother addicted to heroin, her parade of abusive partners and a younger sibling for whom he felt responsible. Sadly his story is not so unusual. Later, back in my warm apartment, I reflected on my own upbringing. Suddenly 'ordinary' seemed more attractive. Yes, there had been some standout episodes but these were mere paragraphs in huge volumes of everyday, commonplace kindness. I had always

DOG LEADS TO GOD

had clean clothes, shoes that fitted, regular meals and set bedtimes, with stories. Like all children, privileged with loving security, I had chafed at the lack of adventure and squealed at perceived hardships. But suddenly 'ordinary' seemed highly appealing. As George Elliot puts it, 'the growing good of the world is partly dependent on unhistoric acts'.[76]

Our dogs might say the same. Their routines are important. They might want to mix things up a bit with new places to sniff out but they still need daily walks. When there is chaos and uncertainty, dogs will become anxious and unstable. Where the basic pattern is predictable and human leadership is constant, they can relax and get on with being dogs. Of course high days and holidays are important, but enjoyment and overexcitement are not synonymous. A giddy dog is not necessarily a happy dog. We might love their crazy antics but that is us projecting human values onto a different species. If wolves dance, they do not do so frenetically. Steady dogs and wild wolves rarely get into those dizzy states which win so many heart-shaped 'likes' on Instagram reels. For dogs, 'ordinary' is good.

I do not know what happened next for that young man, grieving his grandmother. Lack of childhood ordinariness had left him with a shifting sense of right and wrong, anchored not in basic principles but cut adrift in the whims and waves of each moment. Such damage is hard to heal and much careful work needs to be done if decent foundations are to be laid. Mercifully dogs have shorter memories and are more adaptable. Even old dogs can learn new tricks but they will only learn healthy ones under calm leadership where safe routines are ordinary.

We humans are not so different, as we relate to God. Some new converts dive straight in at the deep end while others wade in slowly. All eventually need to explore both the depths and the shallows, if they are to reach spiritual maturity. Sadly those who leap in too quickly, risk leaping out again altogether in search of the next thrill; their thirst for God proven to be more a yearning for adventure. The habits that keep us going (and growing) may at times seem dull: daily prayer, study, giving and meeting for worship. How can such ordinariness bring us closer to a supposedly extraordinary God?

[76] From the closing paragraph of *Middlemarch*, George Eliot

ORDINARY TIME

We could also ask how daily walks, clear boundaries, predictable routines and steady leadership can bring such contentment to our dogs ... but they do.

Something to chew as your dog walks alongside you
Is my 'ordinary' dull or even-keeled? How can I find an ordinary that brings growth without stifling me?

PART 4

LETTING YOUR DOG PACK LEAD YOU TO GOD

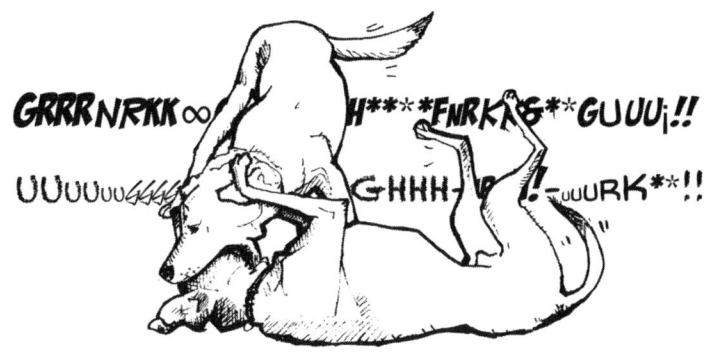

29
IT IS NOT GOOD FOR THE DOG TO BE ALONE

Charlie looked like a happy enough fellow; a handsome, healthy six-year-old Golden Lab, much loved by his humans who provided him with everything he needed: a warm, comfortable home, nutritious food, toys and regular exercise. With hindsight, his lead-guardian describes this phase of Charlie's life as 'two dimensional'. This was not obvious at the time, at least not to any human onlooker. Charlie was not suffering but he was lacking something. This missing 'third dimension' revealed its former absence when the family introduced a puppy, Oscar, to the household and something, previously unsuspected in Charlie awoke.

Imagine living abroad and finally meeting someone who spoke your language. Or being captured by aliens and not seeing another human face for years. There is so much about dogs that we humans do not get and cannot give. We, with our inadequate noses, are hopelessly ill-equipped to catch the rich, complex messages which our dogs so freely exchange. We get shirty when a dog starts sniffing us too enthusiastically and (at least in human terms) inappropriately. But another dog totally gets the ritual and responds with matching

DOG LEADS TO GOD

relish. Charlie, at last, was enjoying some decent nose time.

We can never give the kind of play that truly ignites a dog. Charlie liked a game of fetch well enough but it is rather pallid compared with a full-on canine rumpus. He and Oscar spend an inordinate amount of time, haring around, chewing each other's necks, wrestling and taking turns to submit, all the while grunting and growling in that guttural manner that humans find slightly alarming. You see? We don't even make the right noises.

Oscar benefits too. As a growing pup, he gets a great deal of training from Charlie. It is much easier to follow the example of an obedient older dog, than the confusing instructions of humans. It was not necessarily bad for Charlie to be a lone dog in the house but without a doubt, his new companion has made his life dramatically more fulfilled.

In one of the earliest stories in Genesis, God looks at the newly created Adam and thinks, 'It is not good that the man should be alone'. All the other animals provide company of sorts but they are not enough. Adam needs someone like him and so God creates Eve, from one of Adam's ribs. There is so much to be said at this point but I will limit myself to three things:

1. We do not have room here: for the necessary examination of the patriarchal cultures that recorded and interpreted this story or to do justice to,
2. the scientists who have used DNA to locate a Mitochondrial Eve ... but not an Adam.
3. God is not enough. Humans need other humans. Animal companions are important but they cannot fulfil all our human longings for companionship. Neither can God, not even when God was visible and audible and walked daily with Adam, sharing Eden's evening breeze.[77] God knew this and rectified it.

God did not create pack animals, such as dogs and humans to live isolated from their own kinds. Some guardians have room for only one dog, so they need to set up play dates or find a safe dog-friendly park. And for some humans, marriage is not the right choice or might

[77] Genesis 3:8

IT IS NOT GOOD FOR THE DOG TO BE ALONE

not be possible but enforced loneliness is never a godly alternative. Like Charlie and Oscar, we thrive in partnership and in close contact with others like us. We need God too. But God knows that God is not enough (at least according to how God appears in Genesis). It is not good that the dog should be alone … or the human.

 Something to chew as your dog walks alongside you
How do I meet and balance my needs for companionship: human, divine and canine?

*OR SIT ... OR LIE ... OR NAP ...

30
THERE IS POWER IN THE UNION (OR 'THE PACK')

A meme is doing the rounds. There is a photo of a large crowd of dogs, all different breeds, sizes and ages. The caption reads, 'How you will know that I've won the lottery!' And given a clean slate, no work duties and a large house, how many of us would not fill it with dogs? I said, 'a large crowd' which is a human term. Dogs would call it a pack, which is quite a different thing.

What is the ideal number of dogs? Two is almost always better than one but is it enough? Again we usually approach this question from a human point of view, rightly starting with our resources and asking how many dogs we can accommodate safely. Dogs would say around eight to twelve works well. How do we know this? Because that is the size of the average wolf pack. In the wild these can vary between two and twenty and occasionally contain as many as thirty but let's stick with the average.

A well led pack is a wonderful thing. The top male and female work together to keep the peace and set the direction. Further training happens without classrooms. If the majority are steady their calmness will spread, with new dogs taking their lead from

THERE IS POWER IN THE UNION (OR 'THE PACK')

established members. There might be the odd barked order, snarl or raised hackle but most disputes are resolved without the need for hostility. The pack moves as one. Our own dogs might dilly, dally and delay, taking their time to sniff everything ... or run off, leaving us feeling impotent and frustrated until they deign to return. But when a pack is on the move, the pack sticks together. There is a sense of purpose; lupine leadership is communicated in ways we humans struggle to emulate.

We had a plus-one join our pack for just a week. She began as an extremely fussy eater, shunning cuts of raw meat even when held right before her nose. We did not know how to help her but when she saw Hugo eat, she ran straight to her bowl and got stuck in. On a larger scale, a pack can be healing, the careful immersion of an aggressive dog into a stable pack can teach them how to negotiate respectfully, all the while having their fears calmed. Such operations require skilful supervision from human experts but the actual therapeutic work is done by the pack.

God created both dogs and humans to evolve as pack animals. Unlike snow leopards, moose and platypuses we do not thrive alone. We need others around us. We form trade unions, political parties, sports teams, hobby enthusiasts' clubs, reading groups and even criminal gangs. Christians, if they are to keep the faith, need other Christians. Books, apps, livestreams and downloaded sermons have their place but they are no substitute for face-to-face fellowship. We might not call a parish church a 'pack' but when working well, they both function in many of the same ways: we learn from each other, we bear each other's burdens, we benefit from access to a wider set of skills, we challenge destabilising behaviour so that we can all move forward together. Even hermits belong to communities. Sister Wendy Beckett lived a mostly solitary life but was still a member of a Carmelite monastery.

But there remains a significant difference between our packs and those of wolves; they can smell, see and hear their true leader, whereas ours whilst ever-present, is only visible through the eyes of faith. Belief in God might begin with a personal awakening but it cannot stay as such. We can only grow in the company of others. Jesus points to God as our 'pack leader' and he cautions his followers from imagining anyone else in the alpha slot; titles such as Father, Teacher or Instructor are not for us pack members but for God alone.[78] We are to remain as perpetual students and very much like the dogs in our homes, forever denied a shot at the top job.

Something to chew as your dog walks alongside you
Who is in my pack (or packs)? And how do I benefit from membership? Have I or anyone else, ever tried to assume the top slot?

---

[78] Matthew 23:8-10

31
DOGS DO DIVERSITY

Dogs *usually* mix well with other dogs. They seem to recognise each other as fellow dogs even when they look so different; picture a Chihuahua sitting alongside a Great Dane. Dogs have greater variety in body size, head shape and leg length than any other species of living land animal. American Scientist estimates that the genetic variation between different breeds could be as much as 27.5% (whereas genetic variation amongst human beings is only 5.4%).[79] But despite this, a mixed pack containing several breeds gets along ... usually if not always.

Dog packs might need some help to find their balance. Before norming, there might be some storming while forming but often nothing more serious than a growl or a raised hackle. But when carefully introduced, most dogs, regardless of breed will quickly settle with each other.

It does not stop here. Dogs can do well in packs where diversity includes other species. They positively want to add humans into the mix. And given the right temperament, they can form incredible bonds with cats, pigs, cows and horses. I even found a video of two bulldogs who were best friends with a porcupine.

[79] 'Genetics and the Shape of Dogs', Elaine A. Ostrander, *American Scientist* September-October 2007 Volume 95, Number 5

DOG LEADS TO GOD

Dogs also tolerate different preferences. Some dogs will bolt towards water, launching themselves with gleeful abandon into neighbours swimming pools. Others get all dainty when confronted by a puddle. But here's the thing, whether water-loving or water-loathing, they can coexist happily in the same pack.

Humans are not so good. Many human packs could learn much from their canine counterparts. God made us to be diverse, so it follows that when one group dominates, all miss out on God's gifts. Jesus' team of disciples was far larger than the twelve named males but even when forming that group he chose some very different characters. Today we are still learning the hard way that monochrome, (typically 'male, pale and stale') is never adequate. Former UK Prime Minister, Mr Johnson admitted to the COVID inquiry that his 'top team' could have done better in the pandemic, had it not been so male-dominated.[80] Since 1996 the Harvard Business Review has been advising companies to harness diversity and reshape their power structures accordingly. Add-and-stir-and-hope-for-better-results is not enough; wise companies create *cultures* that refuse inequality. The benefits are evident.[81] Dogs in dog packs know this already. Humans still have some catching up to do.

The good news is that mismatched packs can evolve into well-matched packs and discover unexpected gifts from God. This requires some intelligent negotiating. All benefit when those with power listen to those without. For our households, this means we need to do some imaginative work to ensure our non-verbal pack members are properly heard and understood.

Something to chew as your dog walks alongside you
Is it true that when one group dominates, all miss out on God's gifts?

---

[80] *Ten times Boris Johnson was cornered by Hugo Keith at the Covid inquiry*, Joe Sommerlad, The Independent, December 6, 2023

[81] *Getting Serious About Diversity: Enough Already with the Business Case. It's time for a new way of thinking.* Robin J. Ely and David A. Thomas Harvard Business Review, November to December 2020

CAN WE JUST NOT?

32
ACCEPTING DOGS AS DOGS

When we create a mixed species pack we can forget that dogs are dogs and *not* humans and *certainly not* accessories for humans. Here are three contemporary horror stories:

Handbag dogs: it started with some celebrity posting an image of their new outfit, with a dog sticking its head out of their designer handbag. The trend caught on and certain types of dog, already bred more for appearance than for health, found themselves being carried from one society event to the next. Dogs are dogs, gifted with legs and expected to use their legs. Along with skin diseases, lack of general fitness and problems with socialising, handbags dogs risk being discarded. In 2019 the RSPCA reported a 700% increase over seven years, in the number of chihuahuas being surrendered into their care.[82] French bulldogs, pomeranians and dachshunds fared

[82] *RSPCA begs public to adopt rather than buy dogs as 'designer' and 'handbag' dogs are abandoned in huge numbers*, Rachael Turner, Country Life, 1/10/2019

only marginally better. This is the awful but predictable consequence of treating dogs as fashion accessories. If only it ended here ...

Ear cropping: certain breeds can be 'enhanced' to look more alert, even menacing. Also long ears are a weak spot in any dog destined for fighting. They are cut to remove any flop, leaving them short and sharp like demons' horns. The procedure is usually done when they are still puppies between six and twelve weeks. It is brutal and traumatic. The perpetrators use scissors or a sharp blade but rarely pain relief, inflicting permanent physical and mental damage on their dogs, all in the name of boosting their own inadequate self-image.

Puppy yoga: yep, I had to do a double take but apparently this really is a thing.[83] The puppies don't engage in any of the stretches and positions, they are simply let loose into the room to mingle with the human participants. What could be cuter than doing yoga surrounded by gambolling puppies? Hmm ... But what of puppies' tendency to widdle frequently? That along with all other canine concerns comes secondary to humans having an enhanced experience. Each fresh lycra-clad batch excites the puppies, disrupting their sleep patterns to their long-term detriment. Remember pups need an inordinate amount of sleep. The wee problem is a cruel but easy fix; simply deprive them of water.

The terrible irony is that many of the humans who do these things will self-identify as dog-lovers and will delude themselves with spurious arguments about supposed benefits for the dogs. The simple truth is that we cannot love dogs and treat them as anything other than dogs. Dogs should not be fashion accessories any more than they should be meat for human consumption.

What about us? How have we been made? God never forgets that we are humans, made from dust to flourish for a short time.[84] Laying aside the horrors of binding women's feet and FGM, how often do we impose restrictions upon ourselves to conform our bodies

---

[83] *'Puppy yoga' is on the rise – and as a dog welfare specialist, I'm horrified*, Esme Wheeler, *The Guardian* 13/07/2023
[84] Psalm 103:13-14

ACCEPTING DOGS AS DOGS

to the extremely expensive standards of the surgically augmented? We have created entire industries to improve our appearances with scant regard for any wider consequences; a constant succession of new outfits might help us look better but the Atacama Desert looks far worse now that is has become a dumping ground for unwanted fast fashion.[85] We need to stop being dissatisfied with looking like what we all are: humans who grow older.

Maybe accepting dogs as dogs, in all their variety and difference, might lead us humans to a greater acceptance of self and others and eventually to a fuller understanding of how we are made and loved by God.

Something to chew as your dog walks alongside you
When do my expectations of myself, distort those given by God

[85] *Chile's desert dumping ground for fast fashion leftovers*, Aljazeera, **8 Nov 2021**

Totes ADORBES!! 6d
Reply   See Translation

so sweet 💜☺💜☺💜☺ 1w
Reply   See Translation

what a lovely dog! 3w
Reply   See Translation

For GOD's sake put the damn camera down and get the kid off that poor dog!! 3w
Reply   See Translation

so cute 4w
Reply   See Translation

33
APE KINDNESS VS WOLF KINDNESS

It was not an incident. No one was hurt and it barely lasted a moment. A visiting child, unfamiliar with dogs and intrigued by our Hugo, decided to hug him. Hugo let out a small growl. The child released him at once and then started to cry. But not for long. A parent swooped in, wrapping the child in warm arms, 'No need for those tears. That's just a dog's way of telling you they don't like something.' Lesson learnt and no one hurt.

This was another occasion underlining dogs difference to humans. We ape-descendants offer kindness with hugs. Wolf-descendants do not. Our nearer cousins such as monkeys comfort their frightened young with an embrace. Wolves, jackals, foxes, coyotes do not; their anatomies do not lend themselves to being squeezed. Dogs enjoy touch, such as stroking, cuddling up, scratching and tummy rubs. On a cold winter's evening, our dogs might sleep in a pile but nothing in their long evolution has taught them that being squeezed by strangers is an act of love.

One of my bugbears is video reels of toddlers crawling across the family dog. In my opinion any adult present needs to stop filming

APE KINDNESS VS WOLF KINDNESS

at once and lift said toddler from the dog. But then come the comments: 'Labs are the best!♥♥♥', 'Aw how cute!' 'So sweet.' 'What a lovely dog! ♥☺♥☺♥☺' I scroll down until I find a voice of sanity, 'This dog is showing clear signs of distress. It has no way of saying no.' Actually the dog has, it can growl ... or snap, at which point it instantly becomes the villain when the true culprit is the human twit holding the camera.

Ape-kindness is different from dog-kindness. If we want to be good to our dogs, we need to think beyond our immediate instincts. We apes show love by giving food but we confuse our dogs if we occasionally indulge them from our tables and then complain about them drooling throughout our subsequent meals. As for clothing, humans take pride in our young being well dressed. There is a significant industry cajoling us to spend thousands on outfits for our dogs, even though common sense asserts that they are usually far better off without.

What about God's kindness? Is this closer to wolf kindness or human kindness? God is after all the creator of both. Our (human-written) religious texts tell us that God is more like humans; it is *we* who are made in God's image, not dogs ... or bats or dolphins. All the same, God's ways can be bafflingly strange to us. Where is the kindness in letting a brutal dictator stamp on innocent civilians? How can God tolerate the thriving of billionaires when so many barely survive? And looking beyond human misery, what does the God who made pigs make of our factory farms and abattoirs?

Theologians grapple with God's actions and more often seeming inaction, with varying degrees of helpfulness. C. S. Lewis coined the phrase 'a severe mercy' which another author then adopted as the title of his book describing the death of his beloved wife.[86] Lewis's wisdom helped him but others still struggle. To us apes God can appear at times, unkind. More about this later[87] but for now it is important to note that humans do not know everything about kindness. Dogs, at least often need a different brand.

And what is the kindest thing we can do for our dog? The answer does not involve shopping for new accessories. Dogs do best

[86] *A Severe Mercy*, Sheldon Vanauken, Harper & Row 1977
[87] See chapter 48: 'You're supposed to be in control'

in a pack made up of humans and ideally other (compatible) dogs. We humans certainly give them a lot but a fellow dog can give them so much that we cannot. So if we can, we should expand our pack to include more than one canine companion. And if we are really going all out for kindness then we will take our search, not to a breeder but to the local dog refuge where there is no shortage of willing recipients for wise kindness.

Something to chew as your dog walks alongside you
Has God's kindness ever appeared confusing to me?

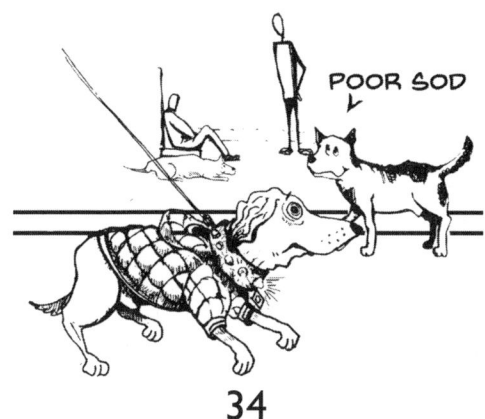

34
THE BEST PACK IN TOWN (FOR DOGS)

Where do we find the happiest dogs? Cesar Millan, better known by his nickname, 'the Dog Whisperer' has a provocative theory.[88] He meets many dogs in his adoptive Los Angeles and believes the steadiest, the calmest, the most contented and fulfilled dogs are those who belong to homeless people.

This is more than a patronising attempt to romanticise the downtrodden. He supplies evidence. Most of his wealthy clients come to him with dogs who will not walk to heel, who tug on their leads, who are aggressive to other dogs and who tear the house apart when left alone. Homeless people's dogs do not behave like this. They suffer little to no separation anxiety because their leaders are usually by their sides. They live in mixed packs, sharing their lives with other canines and humans. If they are ever left alone, it is only for the shortest of times, for instance outside a shop. They are continually on the move, patrolling a wide territory, trotting

[88] *Cesar's Way: The Natural, Everyday Guide to Understanding and Correcting Common Dog Problems*, Cesar Millan with Melissa Jo Peltier, Harmony Books 2006

DOG LEADS TO GOD

alongside their leader. They are rarely bored; they constantly encounter new smells and sights. Most tellingly, they have less need of leads; when their humans move, they move with them, calmly keeping in step. Homeless people's dogs live lives closer to their wolf ancestors than their better housed counterparts.

The pampered pooches of the rich, by contrast, spend far too much time apart from their pack. They may have every human luxury, but being dogs, these are of little value to them: gorgeous houses and designer accessories are human bangles and do nothing to alleviate canine loneliness. Our values are not theirs. They might get taken out at midday by a dog walker, a poor substitute for their actual pack leader, who works long hours, returns too tired for exercise or training and instead of nurturing calmness rewards overexcitement. They positively relish their dog's exuberant welcome failing to spot the anxiety behind it. Some wealthier humans are so focused on being adults in the workplace, that they return to their dogs almost as children needy of parental affection. No wonder their poor dogs are confused.

Our values are not dogs' values. In truth, our values are not our values either. Society drives us towards an 'aspirational life' which is often devoid of certain key essentials, just as ultra-processed food lacks proper nutrition. And yet we persist with our metaphor of choice (the rat race, the grindstone, the corporate ladder) kidding ourselves that we are just one hurdle from happiness. It does not work. Like our dogs, we end up stressed, lonely, anxious and in need of therapy.

We are made by God, for God and for each other. If God made our dogs to be most fulfilled by companionship, work, play and adventure, why would it be so different for us? And why is human society so structured around other things? And yet here is the irony: those most failed by society, own the happiest dogs. What lessons can we learn from them, not only to make us better guardians but better humans?

Jesus taught that we could know what was worthwhile by its fruits.[89] Paul adds to this, by listing the fruits of God's Spirit, 'love, joy, peace, patience, kindness, generosity, faithfulness, gentleness, and

[89] Matthew 7:16

THE BEST PACK IN TOWN (FOR DOGS)

self-control.'[90] Do these work for dogs too? What 'fruit' would be evidence that a dog is walking in step with the Spirit, by whom it was created? Obedience? Nurture of pups? Calmness? ... Completing this list might make a useful 'chew' for your next walk.

> **Something to chew as your dog walks alongside you**
> What 'fruit' would be evidence that a dog is walking in step with the Spirit?

---

[90] Galatians 5:22-23

HOW WE'D LIKE IT TO BE ... BUT SADLY SOMETIMES HOW IT IS

35
WHEN THE PACK NEEDS A RESHUFFLE

Maybe I have been a bit starry eyed about the healing power of a wolf pack. How great if the success rate was 100 per cent? But alas it is not. Some dogs simply cannot live together happily. There comes a time when is better to face facts rather than to persist with a fantasy.

Tinker Bell was a Twilight dog,[91] a feisty soul in an elderly body, rescued after her guardian had died. One of Twilight's supporters visited with her own dog, Mimmi. The two dogs immediately clicked, playing so well that Mimmi's guardian asked whether she might adopt her. All went well at first until Tinker Bell started behaving oddly. It seems that her new and smaller pack, gave her new and larger ideas. She became aggressive towards other dogs. She bit the post deliverer. A change was needed. Without judgement she was brought back to Twilight where she rediscovered her former calm. This had been a worthwhile exercise. Lessons were learnt and no harm was done (apart from to the poor postie). Tinker Bell simply needed a certain type of pack.

[91] More about Twilight tomorrow (by which I mean in the next chapter)

WHEN THE PACK NEEDS A RESHUFFLE

The actor Martin Clunes wrote a book about his life with dogs beginning with his cocker spaniel Mary. After a while he introduced a second cocker, Tina. What looked perfect on paper simply could not work in reality. Tina kept on attacking Mary, not continuously, there were long periods of peace but the attacks when they came were alarming. All sorts of interventions were tried, a third dog was drafted in but in the end the only workable solution was for someone in the wider family to adopt Tina. Both Mary and Tina continued happily, once freed from each other.[92]

What is true for dogs is also true for humans. Some of us do not do well together. Sometimes this is evident from the word go. Sometimes things change and a group that once worked fantastically well has to split. Not all marriages survive. Friendships can end. Churches schism. Even charitable groups can reach a point where faithful members depart.

How is this relevant to God? Surely God's answer is simple? Surely God wants us all to live in love with each other? The Bible extols harmonious relationships.[93] Jesus prayed that his disciples might all be one, and by 'one' he meant enjoying that same unity which he shares with his heavenly Father.[94] This is the ideal but as previously observed, this current world is not the one where the lamb sleeps soundly alongside the wolf.[95]

God is familiar with once-functioning packs ceasing to work. The Bible contains stories of the parting of ways. Paul falls out with his close friend Barnabas in the middle of a missionary journey. The argument was about whether the formerly flaky John Mark should be included on their next trip. Paul, elsewhere an advocate of unity,[96] gives a resolute 'no'. There is no record of the two friends ever meeting again after this.[97]

Love's challenge may be less about aiming for 'best friends forever' and more about refusing to demonise opponents. Jesus insists

[92] *A Dog's Life,* Martin Clunes, Hodder & Stoughton 2009
[93] Psalm 133:1, 'How very good and pleasant it is when kindred live together in unity!'
[94] John 17:21
[95] See chapter 6. Your Kingdom come, on earth as in heaven
[96] Philippians 2:2, Colossians 3:10, Ephesians 4:3
[97] Acts 15:36-41

DOG LEADS TO GOD

on love for enemies.[98] The Quakers interpret this as respecting 'that of God in everyone' and when disagreeing with someone 'always remember[ing] that they too are children of God'.[99] Accepting hard facts, rather than pursuing utopian fantasies does less damage in the long run. It also reduces guilt and by consequence the desire for recriminations. Most humans, most dogs can find a way of rubbing along together but some will never get on.

 Something to chew as your dog walks alongside you
What is God's direction when I encounter someone I sincerely do not like?

---

[98] Matthew 5:43-44
[99] From *Advices & Queries* 1.02 – 17 & 31. The Yearly Meeting of the Religious Society of Friends (Quakers) in Britain © The Yearly Meeting of the Religious Society of Friends (Quakers) in Britain, 1995, 1997 and 2008.

ROO, FALBA & DOBBIE

36
WHAT BECOMES OF THE BROKEN HOUNDS (THE STORY OF AN EXCEPTIONAL PACK)

No one wanted Dobbie. French Bulldogs are usually very popular with prospective guardians but Dobbie's congenital hip disorder and non-functioning hind legs severely reduced his appeal. Added to this, poor Dobbie needs nappies, as he was born with a prolapsed anus and by consequence, faecal incontinence. At just three months old, Dobbie was unadoptable.

Roo is an irrepressible little black smudge of a dog. He was found with a broken back on a busy outer ring road. Whether he was injured while lost, or beforehand and then abandoned is immaterial. He was permanently damaged and unwanted at just eighteen months old.

Falba is a gentle 14-year-old shepherd cross. She embodies the question posed by many older dogs who have been owned by older humans; who wants them when their humans die or become too ill to care for them? Possible adopters are hesitant to invest emotionally in

DOG LEADS TO GOD

a dog who will not be around for long. Then there are the vet's bills. And along with the usual old-age gripes, Falba has dementia.

What becomes of the broken hounds? Who homes the unhomable? There is nothing quite like finding a good answer to these questions. Twilight is a small charity in France's Dordogne.[100] They call themselves a retirement home for dogs but in truth their scope is far wider. Their door stands open for lonely, rejected, sick, damaged and unadoptable dogs. Dobbie, Roo and Falba have all found a safe embrace there. They live in a pack with twenty other dogs and two inspirational humans. Far from being a sad place, it is filled with the kind of joy that draws in an army of volunteers.

Where do broken humans go? What happens to our misfits and rejects? Jesus says that the poor in spirit are welcome in the Kingdom of God,[101] so the obvious place for the otherwise unwanted could be a local church. Sometimes it is (wonderfully so), but at other times, churches are rather too selective about who does and does not belong. They can also become distracted by 'important' duties. Jesus' beatitudes provide no prompts for participation in pomp and pageantry, rather they stand as a call to recognise our common humanity with the easily ignorable. I cannot help feeling that western Churches would not be facing their current decline if they could somehow make Jesus' Sermon on the Mount[102] their 'why' and sit light to everything else, including clinging to unheatable buildings. The joy that comes from living as intended is infectious.

Nancy Pelosi, the 52nd speaker of the United States House of Representatives has the following three words of advice for newly elected senators, 'Know your why.' She recognises how easy it is for any powerful person or institution to lose their 'why'. Amid all the pressures of high office, Speaker Pelosi kept hers firmly at the front of her mind.[103]

Twilight's 'why' is 'ensuring a dog's last memory is of being

---

[100] Twilight, La maison de retraite pour les chiens (www.twilightchiens.com)
[101] Matthew 5:3
[102] Matthew 5-7 and see also Luke 6:20-49
[103] Nancy Pelosi's 'why' is the fact that one in five children in America go to sleep hungry each night. *The Rest is Politics*: Leading podcast, 6/5/24

WHAT BECOMES OF THE BROKEN HOUNDS

loved'. I met Leeanne and Mike, Twilight's mum and dad. I asked Mike how they had started. This soon became a cascade of pup tales. I invited him to tell me a story that began, 'The dog that no one wanted ...' and then realised my error. If Mike had taken me at my word, I would have heard the individual stories of more than four hundred dogs.[104] Instead Mike told me about Dobbie; Dobbie who had stolen their hearts from their first meeting as he bravely dragged himself along, joyfully making the most of his limited life without any trace of self-pity. And then came the day when he found his feet, quite literally. His hind legs started working and he took a walk across the yard.

 Something to chew as your dog walks alongside you
What is the 'why' of the people of God? What is my 'why'?

---

[104] Many of these tales can be found in *Paws Before Bedtime, The story of Twilight* by Association Twilight with Liz Brown

PART 5

LETTING YOUR DOG'S TRAINING LEAD YOU TO GOD

37
'IT'S FOR YOUR OWN GOOD'

Ted hated wearing his cone. He was not all that keen on his medicine either. Both were necessary. He suffered from 'happy tail'; an unusual complaint where a dog damages themselves by wagging too vigorously. The end of the tail splits, opening a wound which then gets infected and cannot heal. Also the walls of Ted's home got spattered with droplets of blood, like scenes from some knee-high slasher movie.

In the end Ted's tail had to be docked. After the operation his guardian, Chris used up all his annual leave so that Ted was never left alone. He moved his mattress downstairs to keep him company through the night. Even so, along with his hated cone, Ted had to be muzzled and sedated to keep him from reopening his wound. How to explain to him, 'All this, it's for your own good'?

This brings us onto tricky ground with God. The direct parallel should be simple: we require our dogs to swallow pills they would rather not, we hold their heads still to remove ticks and we restrain them as we train them, to keep them safe. Does God in like manner train, correct and restrain us 'for our own good'?[105] We read how God is the gardener who prunes unfruitful branches.[106] The Bible's authors also warn us that our training will be unwelcome initially,

> Now, discipline always seems painful rather than pleasant at the time, but later it yields the peaceful fruit of righteousness to those who have been trained by it.[107]

So far, so sensible. Trouble comes when some humans claiming to act for God, impose unwarranted corrections onto other humans and label these 'for your own good'. We can be exceptionally bad at this, misdiagnosing innocent states and dispensing appalling interventions; I am thinking of Inquisitions (with a capital 'I') witch-hunts, re-education camps, botched exorcisms, the silencing of women and conversion therapies for LGBTQ+ people.

Correction (when needed) and training are important but they *must* be the right sort. Untrained dogs generally live frustrated lives. Ill-disciplined humans are also unhappy and spread their unhappiness around. If we consider the world's assembled leaders, we can quickly spot those who as children never learnt the word 'no' and as 'adults' refuse the medicine of critical self-awareness. I cannot imagine certain premiers ever entertaining the Quakers' advice, 'Think it possible that you may be mistaken'[108] or understand when both Taylor Swift and G. K. Chesterton identify themselves as 'the problem'.[109]

Does God ever do things to us, adding the explanation, 'it's for your own good'? If so, how can we be sure it really is God rather than

---

[105] Deuteronomy 8:5, Revelation 3:19
[106] John 15:2
[107] Hebrews 12:11 and see also the wider context of Hebrews 12:5-11 and Job 5:17, Psalm 94:12,
[108] From *Advices & Queries* 1.02 – 17. The Yearly Meeting of the Religious Society of Friends (Quakers) in Britain © The Yearly Meeting of the Religious Society of Friends (Quakers) in Britain, 1995, 1997 and 2008.
[109] There is an enduring story that G. K. Chesterton famously answered the question in the Times, 'What is wrong with the world?' with, 'Dear Sir, I am.' Taylor Swift's song 'Anti Hero' (Midnights, Republic Records, 2022) makes a similar admission.

'IT'S FOR YOUR OWN GOOD'

some human weaponising out-of-context Bible verses? Remember, a dog's anti-scratch head cone looks remarkably like the women's bonnet in *The Handmaid's Tale*, both nominally imposed 'for your own good', one genuinely is and the other is definitely not. But how can we discern the difference? And how can we ensure the training we give our dogs really is for *their* benefit?

 Something to chew as your dog walks alongside you
What does a genuine rebuke from God feel like?

38
STEADINESS

A nun, a priest, a dog trainer and an ancient Hebrew prophet walk into a bar ... and find they are (sadly) not in a joke but rather in a conversation about understanding dogs.

Sister Julienne, fictional nun and midwife, cuts through all the complexities of 1950s East London life with a very simple observation; there are only ever two reasons behind any choice, love or fear (and sometimes a mixture of both).[110]

Reverend Jo Calladine, real-life priest and prison chaplain, maintains that anger is only ever a secondary emotion and we always need to look beyond for the primary (which is usually fear).

And what is true for humans is also true for dogs. The reason for aggression? Fear, perhaps the legacy of a traumatic event in the past. Destructive behaviour? Again born of fear; a dog that destroys things when left alone, is anxious of being abandoned. Incontinence? Anxiety and bladder control can be closely linked. Hyperactivity and hyper-alertness? Symptoms that a dog does not feel safe. And so on. Could all the principles of dog training come down to Sister

[110] *Call the Midwife*, season 2, Christmas Special (first broadcast 25 December 2012) BBC.

STEADINESS

Julienne's one simple observation; that dogs, like humans, act primarily out of love and fear?

Cesar Millan, the 'Dog whisperer', says that the ideal human for any dog, is calm and assertive.[111] Dogs respond well when their humans are gentle, firm, collected and very much in charge. He has made a successful business and achieved stardom by being that person around dogs, especially dogs rejected as too damaged and too difficult to be comfortably homed.

Perhaps we should rebrand aggressive dogs as 'anxious'. Beneath the bravado quivers a frightened puppy, trying to take charge in an unsafe world. There are three standard responses to threat: fight, flight or freeze. Unsteady dogs opt for different combinations of these. There is a fourth option, only available to those who are gaining steadiness, which is calm trust or to continue the alliteration … faith. When their training is calm, dogs learn trust and in time, trade their anxiety for faith in their human leader.

> The prophet Isaiah also believed in steadiness. He said to God, 'Those of steadfast mind you keep in peace – in peace because they trust in you'.[112]

Humans who live by fear, are unhappy. Humans who routinely swap fear for well-placed trust are a delight. Some find that God can be their calm assertive guardian who replaces surrendered troubles with a peace beyond understanding.[113] Sadly, it does not follow that all religious people are well adapted, lovely and lovable. Some of the nastiest humans are also frantically religious and too many religious systems shamelessly exacerbate fears, painting God as a petty, peevish, vengeful tyrant, all the better to coerce their flocks. Survivors of such abuse require help untangling all this before they are able to wholeheartedly agree with St John, that, 'God is love, and

---

[111] *Cesar's Way: The Natural, Everyday Guide to Understanding and Correcting Common Dog Problems*, Cesar Millan with Melissa Jo Peltier, Harmony Books 2006
[112] Isaiah 26:3
[113] Philippians 4:7

DOG LEADS TO GOD

those who abide in love abide in God, and God abides in them.'[114]

As we will see throughout this current section, all worthwhile training requires steadiness: terrified dogs and anxious humans will always be erratic and veer to extremes but those who find steadiness thrive.

 Something to chew as your dog walks alongside you
When have I known steadiness in my life? And whom do I see demonstrating calm assertiveness?

---

[114] 1 John 4:16

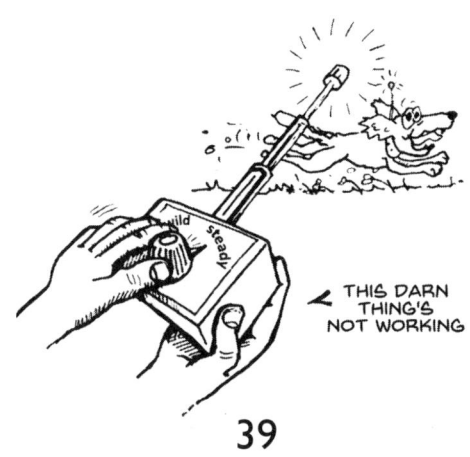

39
HELPING YOUR DOG TO GROW IN 'STEADINESS'

A mother, frazzled after queuing for two long hours, finally places her three-year-old on Father Christmas's knee. She threatens the now terrified, sobbing child, 'If you don't stop that noise and start enjoying yourself and smile for the camera, I'll …!'

This is not going to work. The final photo will only ever evoke memories of frustration rather than the intended warm glow. Some days nothing goes as planned. The storybook ending just isn't going to happen. Some days we need to accept failure, go to bed early and on waking return to the drawing board.

This same dynamic exists with our dogs and their training. Of course we want them to behave well. Poor behaviour can be exasperating, not least because it reflects badly on us, their guardians. No sensible person would argue for an uber-tolerant approach where we passively observe our dogs bounding around the park, knocking over strangers and harassing other dogs. We have a very clear duty to control them but this will never be achieved by bellowing. If yesterday's reading was correct, then the prime driver for any poor behaviour is fear. And calming fears by yelling is as

DOG LEADS TO GOD

counterproductive as threatening a child to cheer up.

I often wish there was a 'steadiness switch' somewhere on our dogs. Then whenever we encounter the kind of situation that sends them into orbit, we could with one deft click, ensure that we would continue calmly without incident. While we're fantasising about the impossible, we might also add to the list a 'holiness switch' for ourselves; a celestial override button which when pressed would instantly return us to the state where we are most mindful of God and thus prevent our straying into regrettable behaviour. No one, however, gets holy in a hurry; sanctimonious maybe, but holy? No. There are no short cuts or accelerated programs, just the patient disciplines of regular prayer, meditation, study, service, almsgiving and fellowship over months and years. *And* the further along we get, the greater the road ahead seems. In this life, God has no graduates, we all remain as perpetual learners, as prone to returning to square one as any dog caught off guard by a bolting rabbit.

Achieving steadiness for dogs requires much patience from all parties involved. There is no substitute for regular walks, playtimes, affirmation, praise and treats from a calm and confident leader. As with holiness, there will be epiphanies and breakthroughs, followed by crashes and disappointments. If we can learn to love our dogs wherever they are on this journey, maybe we can glimpse how much God loves us as we stumble along, distractedly on ours.

God is sometimes imagined, in the Bible and by later preachers, as a yelling God, appalled at our human fascination with the regrettable. But like a periodically reappearing golden thread, Scripture contains another view: a gentle, patient God, who does not break bruised reeds nor snuff out dimly burning candle wicks,[115] a God who is slow to anger and abounds in steadfast love.[116] John the Baptist expected God to send someone rather shouty,[117] but when Jesus finally appeared, he struck a previously unreached balance of gentleness, firmness and fairness. Perhaps we can aspire to such grace as we train our dogs.

---

[115] Isaiah 42:3
[116] Psalm 86:15
[117] Matthew 3:12

HELPING YOUR DOG TO GROW IN 'STEADINESS'

 Something to chew as your dog walks alongside you
How does 'growing in holiness' sound? Exciting? Stultifying? Enriching? Diminishing? Or some other feeling?

40
LITTLE AND OFTEN

How's the new regime going? | Are you being realistic? | I love your enthusiasm but remember, your rigorous routines won't produce immediate results, so don't get discouraged. | Lasting change takes time. | Stick at it and you'll get there.

The above could said to someone who is: 1. puppy training 2. losing weight or 3. growing in faith. None of which are quick processes … nor smooth … an otherwise excellent day can crash with a scuffle with another dog, an empty ice cream tub or a petulant burst of self-righteous anger (depending on which discipline we are attempting).

Training a dog seems to take forever. I am tempted to argue with ours, 'But you *do* know what to do. We've been through this so many times. And you got it right yesterday. How come you've forgotten it all today?' The current task is all about not lunging while out on the lead. Fortunately I have an expert trainer who reminds me to stick to single word commands and patiently repeat these until the dog responds. She has noticed other things too, for instance when he leaps ahead, I cry 'STOP' and when he does, he stands still waiting for me to catch up. 'Try something new,' she offered, 'how about you stay where you are. Don't tug on the lead just calmly call

LITTLE AND OFTEN

him back to you. Maybe even take a few steps backwards yourself. Get *him* to correct the error. And when he does reward him.' I must have frowned because she then added the encouragement, 'This will help him learn'. In truth, I was thinking, 'If we do it your way, we'll never get anywhere. It'll be a constant stop-start, stop-start, stop-start ... and I'll run out of treats.' And I was right ... and then so was she. Initially our walks were reduced to a painful crawl but gradually things are picking up, increasingly the lead hangs in that desired U-shape and we all find ourselves distinctly calmer. We are still very far from 'there'. And maybe we never will reach a state of perfect obedience but the last time he locked his eyes on a startled deer, he did not immediately launch himself after it. And that's something.

Little and often seems to be the way. We are playing a long, slow game starting at 'very small' and building from there. If I could, I'd cram it all into a boot camp and achieve perfection in ten days but neither dog-training nor dieting work like that. Small, doable, incremental changes are the way forward. A friend, a weary father of four has the following mantra, 'Discipline is a culture not an instant.'

This also applies to any who wish to grow with God. As said before, no one gets holy in a hurry. Some might be more adept at finding saintly masks but given sufficient provocation, these will slip and reveal a truer picture of their progress. We should not be disheartened by the stop-start, one-step-forward-two-steps-back nature of our journey. Reading the gospels is a good antidote to discouragement, noting Jesus' patience with the antics of the first disciples. They lived face to face with Jesus and *still* got things hopelessly muddled. Worthwhile development is slow. We are unlikely to appreciate the changes; relatives are more aware of children's growth than their parents and visitors sometimes comment on a dog, 'He's so much calmer than he was last year.' All such encouragement is good. We might not notice otherwise.

And if we are really lucky there might be a double win: our dog grows in steadiness as we grow in kindness, joy and patience; patience most of all, because none of this is going to happen overnight.

Something to chew as your dog walks alongside you
How good am I with patience? How might I grow this fruit?

41
DISTRACTIONS

How can we expect our dogs to grow in steadiness when we ourselves are so easily distracted? Some days I cannot sit in prayerful contemplation for even five seconds without my mind boarding some random passing train of thought and zipping off on a cross country rampage, taking me miles from my intended destination.

But is distraction always a bad thing? Certainly not in dog training; used correctly it can be an essential tool. Think of those times when your dog has slammed on the brakes and refused to budge, fixated by something they have seen or smelled? What to do when our dogs are heading for 'the Zone'?[118] Remembering that the longer we delay, the deeper in they go.

This is when distraction becomes our ally. We begin with our voice but if that does not provide sufficient distraction, we can try a gentle tug on the lead and failing that, we resort to treats. I have taken to carrying a bag of kibbles on all our walks. Often just rattling is enough to break the spell but if not, I scatter a couple on the ground. This has a 99 per cent success rate.

---

[118] For more about 'the Zone' see chapters 4-7 of *The Dog Walker's Guide to God*.

DOG LEADS TO GOD

The distraction of food to be snuffled out overrides most other distractions.

How can this dog anecdote lead us to God, and especially on those days when praying and meditating is little more than a battle against distractions? Here is a cure: find one single distraction to distract from all the other distractions and then allow God's calm to descend. Food trumps most things with our dogs, so what is its equivalent for us humans? Fortunately many have already asked this question and left us a wealth of useful answers.

A focus on breathing is tried and tested. Across many different religious traditions, concentrating the mind on breath entering and breath leaving the body, draws us away from our legion of distractions and calms our whole system.

Some add a prayer word, a phrase or mantra, letting its repetition act as a sponge to soak up any lingering wannabe distractions.

Others find that concentrating on a candle's flame brings the same benefit.

Posture is also important. I require my dogs to sit or lie down as part of their calming process. We humans do well to find which physical positions work best for us. Some aim for complete stillness while others are soothed by the rhythm of walking. The more flexible might sit cross legged or kneel. One consistent piece of advice is that slumping is to be avoided. A back which is as straight as possible, allows air to flow in and out with greater ease; it is hard for our bodies to release tension when struggling for breath. We need to aim for something which is both relaxed and alert (and if you want to know how to do alert, rustle a treat bag and then mimic your dog's posture.)

As said before, little and often is key; progress rarely comes in great leaps. But the day will come when your formerly lurching dog will calmly walk with you past barking dogs with barely a twitch. They will spot a hare but then quickly return their attention to you. And we too might find that we can sit with God, sharing the 'silence of eternity' for a few more seconds ... and maybe even a little bit longer.

DISTRACTIONS

 Something to chew as your dog walks alongside you
Have I found the one single distraction which distracts my dog from all the other distractions? And have I found the same for myself?

BlueSniff   NoseBook

Instawhiff   NoseTime

42
NOSETIME: HOW MUCH IS TOO MUCH?

Do your dog walks flow freely? Or are they a constant stop-start due to your dog jolting you to an abrupt halt every single time something catches their nose?

Dogs are not addicted to social media but if there were computers designed for them, they would have apps called NoseBook, NoseTime, Instawhiff, BlueSniff and X (which everyone still calls Sniffer). We humans glue our eyes to screens, occasionally laughing, sometimes fuming and quite often bored ... but still scrolling on in the hope that the next reel will deliver a better dopamine hit than the last. Dogs have a much healthier way of keeping up with each other, through scent. When physically present they sniff each other's anal glands and when distant they also examine posts ... fence posts and door posts and anything else that can be peed against; their urine containing a rich repository of revealing material for those with noses to smell.

Information enters the nose, is captured and then transmitted to the brain for analysis. The *process* is the same for humans and dogs but the *priority* is different. Dogs engage with the world nose

NOSETIME: HOW MUCH IS TOO MUCH?

first. A human nose contains five million scent receptors whereas a dog's nose has between one hundred and twenty-five million and three hundred million, depending on breed with bloodhounds and beagles leading the pack. Even small dogs' noses far outstrip our human snouts.

Sniffed information travels from these receptors via nerves to olfactory bulbs at the front of the brain. A human's combined bulbs weigh about fifteen grams, a dog's weigh around sixty grams.[119] Given all this equipment for gathering and processing scent, it should be no surprise that dogs are prone to distraction to the point of addiction when out walking.

It takes Barry almost an hour to walk Barney. Freda gets it done in twenty minutes. Barry lets Barney stop and sniff as much as he likes, 'Dogs like smelling. That's what gives them pleasure. I'm just letting my dog be a dog.' Freda takes a different tack, 'It's important the dog knows who's in charge. I'm not letting his nose dictate to me. He's compulsive. I'm not going to indulge that. When we're out, he walks to heel. If he wants to sniff things, he can do it in his own time in the garden and without yanking my arm.'

Freda and Barry have a daughter, Maisie. Freda believes it's good that Maisie keeps up with so many friends, 'You'll never believe how many followers she's got on Instagram.' Barry says, 'She should put that damn phone down, go out and get some fresh air. Why can't she actually meet her so-called friends in person? And I'll say it again, all phones are banned at the table when we're eating.'

Barry and Freda make some good points for both Barney and Maisie ... and then some less good ones. If they worked together, they might find a goldilocks zone. Maisie needs some help with self-control. Barney needs to exercise and sniff but not in a way that ruins the walk for his humans. If he were a wolf, the roaming pack would be neither as restrictive as Freda nor as indulgent as Barry; a wolf that stops to sniff too often might get left behind. Balance is the thing and in both cases, Freda and Barry have key roles.

Some religious people might pride themselves on not being addicted to anything including social media and any other human

[119] Page 51, *How Dogs Think: What the World Looks Like to Them and Why They Act the Way They Do*, Stanley Coren, Atria 2005

DOG LEADS TO GOD

comparators to excessive sniffing. But religious addiction is also a thing. Jesus says, 'strive first for the Kingdom of God'[120] and St Paul encourages Christians to offer themselves as 'living sacrifices' to God[121] both of which sayings are highly commendable ... for those with healthy, holistic views of God and of the life God gives us. Those less fortunate might find themselves on a treadmill, exhausted and unable to placate a god who despises weakness while ever demanding more and more. The symptoms are varied: anxiety, compulsive adherence to religious routines, alarm at curiosity, suspicion of the new, judgement of divergence, isolation from former friends, guilt and shame.

A good question to ask ourselves is, 'My sense of fulfilment comes from ...?' A warning bell should ring if our answers lean too heavily on *our activity* (for God). A further bell should ring even louder if we find ourselves feeling superior to others. Smugness is not a virtue. Any 'God given' platform from which we can look down on others, is not given by God. If our answers are about *God's activity* for us and if our general default is gratitude mixed with affection towards others then we are probably doing okay. Barney and Maisie could both benefit from an examination of the anxieties that drive their compulsions. And if ever we find ourselves getting obsessive, we could do the same.

 Something to chew as your dog walks alongside you
My sense of fulfilment comes from ...?

---

[120] Matthew 6:33
[121] Romans 12:1

PART 6

LETTING DOG WORK LEAD YOU TO GOD

43
FINDING FOOD IS WORK ... WOLF WORK

Dog work is a pejorative term but it should not be so, there is dignity in work. Sadly unemployment is rife among dogs. At some point in our recent history, the majority of western dogs lost their jobs and moved into the ranks of the stay-at-home/permanently-off-work. This transition was made with very little thought for our dogs' well-being.

At the start of the twentieth century dogs earned their keep. By the end many Akitas, Mastiffs and Boxers no longer hunted for big game or even any game, Schnauzers barked at suburban front doors rather than around the fences of Swiss farms, Newfoundlands were no longer needed on ships and there were fewer sleds for Huskies to pull. Humans, having developed these different breeds, switched to machines and carelessly expected their companions simply to drop all their inherited instincts. Mercifully adult dogs sleep for around sixteen hours a day but during the other eight they have an inbred need to be doing purposeful things.

Unemployment is no fun for humans. We get bored. We lose confidence. We reduce our expectations for what we can achieve.

DOG LEADS TO GOD

As we lose a sense of control over our own lives we might seek to compensate by inappropriately controlling others. We should not be surprised if we observe similar deteriorations in our dogs. Conversely our dogs will thrive, physically, mentally *and* in terms of steadiness if we can get them feeling gainfully employed.

The good news is that there are plenty of 'jobs' we can give to our dogs and better still, many of these jobs will feel like play to us. Feeding is the most obvious starting point. Wolves (and their dog descendants) expect to work for their food. Scavenging and hunting are wolf work. Imagine what food is like for a wolf pack; the planning and execution of hunts, the excitement, the danger, the adrenalin, the pounding blood, the moment of capture, the satiation, the correlation of exercise and reward ... and then compare all this to being presented twice daily with a bowl of moist kibbles. So why not make your dogs work for their dinner? I am not suggesting a resumption of hunting; most humans (including dedicated meat-lovers) are far too squeamish for such gory realities. But if you have a garden, try hiding some food and then letting the dog out to find it. Leave trails of biscuits in long grass or scatter them across a lawn. This is counterintuitive; it would be such an ungracious way to serve meals to fellow humans but dogs are not humans, they are dogs. Watch their tails while they forage. Such games will get your dogs' brains working and afterwards leave them satisfied by a job well done, maybe as we are at the end of a well-spent, fruitful day.

There is dignity in work. We might fantasise about a life of ease, surrounded by flunkies anticipating our every whim. In truth, most of us would tire of this pretty quickly. Why? Because God has not designed us to be so pampered. God intended us to work. In the Book of Genesis, one of the creation stories sees Adam being set to work first tilling the Garden of Eden and then naming all the animals.[122] Work is good. Not that God created us for an eternity of clocking in and slogging away until collapsing into an early death. That is toil and 'toil' is what work becomes only after the Fall: 'By the sweat of your face, you shall eat bread until you return to the ground.'[123]

[122] Genesis 2:15-19
[123] See Genesis 3:17-19

FINDING FOOD IS WORK ... WOLF WORK

True work satisfies. God made neither humans nor dogs for unemployment.

 Something to chew as your dog walks alongside you
Does the prospect of work, especially work for God excite me or leave me feeling drained? If the latter, what might I change?

44
WALKS ARE WORK ... WOLF WORK (i)

Every so often if we're lucky, we find a job which gives us this sense, 'I was made for this. This work, this moment, this is me being what God made me to be.' This might come to: a footballer walking out onto a pitch, a priest standing behind her altar, a carpenter joining together their perfectly cut pieces of wood, a nurse seeing a patient respond to treatment. Vincent van Gogh found this when painting. In a letter to his brother, he describes a transcendent moment, 'And then my brush, between my fingers becomes as a bow on a violin and plays absolutely for my pleasure.'[124]

My hunch is that dogs when they are out walking will be sensing (if not actually thinking) along similar lines, 'This is what I was made to do ... walking for miles ... me with my leader and my pack. This just feels right. This is me being me, us being us living our best dog-life.'

I once thought that what humans call 'a walk' dogs might call 'a sniff', that seeming to be their priority. I even considered writing

---

[124] *The Letters of Vincent van Gogh*, Letter 607 (805), to his brother Theo, c. 19/9/1889

WALKS ARE WORK ... WOLF WORK (i)

a chapter called, 'sniffies not walkies'. I am so glad I did not since it is a false dichotomy. Just one fact turned my all thinking right way up: wolves spend around eight hours a day walking, travelling as far as thirty miles. Repressing a slight cringe about the much shorter strolls I afford my pooches, I read on. Each year in September, the new pups at six months old, participate fully in these massive hikes. Long walks are instinctive, hardwired into lupine (and therefore canine) DNA.

So what do wolves do when out walking or rather trotting along at around five miles an hour? Hunting and sniffing both come into it but there is more. Walking is also exploring, defending even expanding their territories, which can be as large as five hundred square miles. This would explain why our dogs get so excited when we reach for their leads, 'At last! We're about to do all those things we're supposed to be doing! Work! Dignity! Purpose!" And equally, it's no wonder they become frustrated if their daily exercise is little more than a quick once-around-the-block or being let out into the yard to pee and poo. And pity those poor mutts permanently chained up!

In a dog-centric world, they would be out with their leader for hours at a time. The human-centric world is entirely unsuitable for such wolf work. To us a big garden looks ideal but to dogs a couple of fenced-off acres looks paltry compared with the hundred or so square miles that their wolf genes expect. We ape-descended bipeds value our traffic and livestock far over our dogs' optimum selves, so we make it impossible for them to roam where they will. Our pallid 'walkies' may never fully sate their lupine desires but we can console them (and ourselves) with another fact; wolves' lives are hard and short, those that survive to adulthood might manage five years, pack leaders sometimes as many as nine, whereas we expect our domestic dogs to be around for thirteen or more years. If our dogs understood this, would they feel they had the better deal? Or would they feel jealous of their wider-roaming wolf cousins?

God seems to give us various jobs at different times in our lives. It can be hard to discern exactly what God is inviting us to. Sometimes a feeling of unease or restlessness can be God's Spirit prompting us to move on. But when we find ourselves in the right place ... goodness me! That purposeful peace is like nothing else. 'This is what God made me to do ... to be!' I believe our primary call is less about our activities and more about simply being ourselves before God, knowing we are held in God's gaze of love. And if we are really lucky, we might find ourselves out on a path, enjoying God's presence with our dogs trotting alongside us, all of us agreeing, 'We were made for this.'

Something to chew as your dog walks alongside you

Have I ever felt, '*This* is what God made me for'?

45
WALKS ARE WORK ... WOLF WORK (ii)

A pair of dogs live nearby; one white, the other brown. They are largish and the white one has something of a bulldog look to its face. The moment I see them I turn the other way and start texting friends. They roam unsupervised, appearing every couple of months trotting around the village, tails high and bright eyed. They have a reputation for attacking cats and poultry. Countless complaints have been put in but our local authorities refuse to confront the guardians. Possibly they are waiting for the kind of disaster that can be incontrovertibly pinned upon them before taking action.

A pair of dogs live nearby; one white, the other brown. They have a wretched existence. They are given no regular exercise. They are kept locked up in a muddy yard. Their humans do not feed them properly. Discipline is mostly non-existent but sporadically harsh. At least they have each other. Every so often they manage to break out and savour the sweetness, not just of freedom but also of that sense of being their true selves, of working purposefully, of answering the deep call of their wolf genes to explore their territory. They cover miles and miles, checking in on a wide variety of different locations.

DOG LEADS TO GOD

And if they are really lucky, they will find something to chase before some human comes and spoils it all, by returning them to their miserable compound.

Two very different perspectives on one situation but there is a patch of common ground: the humans who call themselves the 'guardians' of these two dogs, are failing everyone, the dogs included.

If you can find a local map on the internet or better still a paper map, pinpoint your home and draw a circle around it, with an approximately eleven-mile diameter. Look at the terrain enclosed. There might be a river or a pond, high points and troughs, woodland and open spaces. All of this, given free range, is what your dog's DNA would claim as theirs. They would form a pack and walk this territory, patrolling by stages, every step of the entire thirty-six-mile circumference at least once a month. However in our human world, many other dogs live within this large circle, all aspiring to similar territorial claims. Also on your map, note the paths, parks, houses, gardens, factories, graveyards, shopping streets, industrial estates, golf courses, railways and roads, some of which are dangerously busy. Dogs share their world with a species that seriously constricts their 'wolf work'.

None of us can do whatever we want whenever the mood takes us. We are often denied our potential or blocked from work that truly satisfies. Dogs and humans alike have to live with restrictions, enforced by others. Even wolves cannot roam wherever they please; along with humans, rival packs impose limits on them, fighting with them over contested ground.

How does all this tally with a loving Creator? What does God wish for us? For humans to dominate all other species, ensuring nothing stands in the way of human progress? Or for all to find ways of living more harmoniously, respectfully allowing each other as much freedom as possible? The latter seems better. And since God has given humans far greater intelligence and far better communication skills than any other animal, the lead surely is ours (at least until the Kingdom comes in all its fullness).

Unfortunately we are not good at living peacefully even within our own species. We place shocking restrictions on other humans according to differences in race, gender, religion, sexuality, ability

WALKS ARE WORK ... WOLF WORK (ii)

and wealth and that is just the start of a much longer list. Those higher up the chain, experience fewer limitations and often dismiss the testimonies of those lower down. (James O' Brien observes that those born three nil up often parade around like they've scored a hat-trick!) How does our confining of others tally with our belief in a loving God? The answer is 'not well.' While we have cars and livestock, we can never permit our dogs to run free. But why do we persist in so restricting our fellow humans?

Something to chew as your dog walks alongside you

How can I live in greater harmony with the rest of God's creation?

PART 7

LETTING SOMETHING SAID ABOUT DOGS LEAD YOU TO GOD

46

'HE'S NEVER DONE THAT BEFORE'

'He's never done that before.' I said truthfully if weakly on top of Pendle Hill. My dog (now long departed) had just launched an unprovoked attacked on a small Yorkie whose guardians were justifiably upset. This came out of the blue. Up to this point he had always been good with other dogs.

New things can be alarming but are they always dangerous?

'They've never done that before!' our dogs said the first time they saw us getting into a swimming pool. A better translation of their berserk barking would be, 'Stop! This is madness! Stop it NOW!' as they pelted round and round the edge, scolding us to climb out. Had we been able to reason with them, we would have explained that swimming may be new to them but we have been doing this from long before they were conceived. I doubt that would have convinced them and stopped them repeating 'Don't blame us for getting upset when you do things we've never seen before!'

What about 'God's never done that before'? How do we react to the prospect of God doing something new? Do we welcome it or dismiss the very notion? When the prophet Isaiah heard God

DOG LEADS TO GOD

speaking about a new direction rather than freaking out, he reported God's words, 'I am about to do a new thing; now it springs forth, do you not perceive it? I will make a way in the wilderness and rivers in the desert.'[125]

Some Christians consider that all we need of God has been fully revealed already. New insights, new divine activities were discovered as the Scriptures were being written but now, no more is needed as all was completed in Jesus, God's final prophet and definitive self-revelation. Paul and others added some further explanatory writings and then the canon was closed. So unlike Isaiah way back when, we should not be looking for new things now. Our task today, is to understand God's full self-revelation in Jesus and live faithfully in accordance.

Other Christians hold that the book is still open. God is still capable of surprising us with new things or at least with things that seem new to us. Our job is to strike a balance, being neither scared nor gullible but open to whatever God is doing now. We should 'test the spirits to see whether they are from God'.[126]

Both positions have their problems. The former risks being hidebound, restricting us with a theology from a very different age and culture. Why would God want us to be limited by the writings of those who did not understand fossils, bacteria, mental health or the patriarchal system in which they lived? The latter risks being built on shifting sands if it swaps the foundational rock of Jesus' teaching for the passing fads of today, leaving a well-meaning but self-serving, quasi-Christian religion centred around a God fashioned to look very much like us.

I wonder what God makes of it all. In my fifties I am less cautious of the new than I was in my twenties. AI alarms me but when it comes to other 'new things' ... women taking a lead, gay people getting married, disabled people expecting equality and structural racism being identified and overturned, I feel no need to run around the pool, barking in panic and protesting, 'This can't be of God because God's never done that before'. Maybe these are completely new things. Or maybe only new to us if God has been intending

[125] Isaiah 43:19
[126] 1 John 4:1

'HE'S NEVER DONE THAT BEFORE'

them from long before any of us were conceived. And maybe, in the new Jerusalem when God speaks from the throne saying 'See, I am making all things new,[127] 'new' will mean new and even better than merely an improvement of what has already been given. Maybe.

Something to chew as your dog walks alongside you
A Quaker's question, 'Are you open to new light, from whatever source it may come? Do you approach new ideas with discernment?'[128]

---

[127] Revelation 21:5
[128] From *Advices & Queries* 1.02 – 7. The Yearly Meeting of the Religious Society of Friends (Quakers) in Britain, © The Yearly Meeting of the Religious Society of Friends (Quakers) in Britain, 1995, 1997 and 2008.

47

'WILL YOU STOP BARKING!'

It great when dogs protect us but less so when they are overprotective. A strange dog being walked past our home is not a threat so we don't need the whole barking, bouncing, snarling display. But protection was a key element in the wolf pact which our ancestors made all those thousands of years ago: we feed and shelter our dogs and in return they alert us to potential danger and attack those who attack us.

I once witnessed a scene. A group of teenagers were messing about, teasing and jibing at each other. A watching mother said, 'Take it down a notch, the dog is getting confused.' The teenagers ignored her. As the horseplay continued, one hoisted her daughter in a fireman's lift. Immediately the dog leapt up and nipped his arm, drawing blood. The boy dropped her, shaken. The mother shrugged, 'I warned you. And DON'T blame the dog for being a dog and doing his job.'

Here's a question ... and I cannot settle on just one answer. Do we have a duty to protect God? John Calvin certainly thought so: 'A dog barks when his master is attacked. I would be a coward if I saw that God's truth is attacked and yet would remain silent.'

'WILL YOU STOP BARKING!'

His reasoning wins bonus points from me because he uses a dog-based *qal wahomer* argument; if this small thing is true in my dogs' relationship to me, how much more might it be true between me and God?

I am all for a bit of barking when there is danger approaching people, animals and planet. I also want to protect certain concepts, such as public truth. I do a lot of panicked yapping when certain politicians lie and lie and lie, to sell us a dubious policy or to wangle their way out of an awkward moment. But is defending public truth the same as protecting God? Read Calvin's quotation again; was he concerned for God his master or for God's truth or for truth in general? Or maybe he saw no difference?

Some religious people perceive a criticism of their holy book as a direct attack on their God. In their fight to save God's reputation, the 'holiness' of their end is often cited to justify some worryingly unholy means. But we cannot honour God with dirty tactics. And we need to be honest; are we protesting an assault on God, are we trying to protect God's people or are we reacting to a threat on our own influence?

The comedian Jeremy Hardy cautioned his critics from roping God into their outrage. He reasoned that if God is God, then God can handle offence and furthermore, not one, of the many, many complaints he had received about blasphemy, had ever come from God, only from humans presuming to speak for God.[129]

Is God ever in danger? Do we have a duty to bark and even bite to 'save' God? What does God make of our offers of protection? Do we imagine gratitude? Or maybe a wry smile when we've misunderstood a situation? How about when our zeal to defend, leads us to cross an ethical boundary? Is God still smiling?

 Something to chew as your dog walks alongside you
Does God ever need our protection?

---

[129] 'Jeremy Hardy Speaks to the Nation', *How to Be Yourself*, 5:1, BBC Radio 4, 2003

48
'YOU'RE SUPPOSED TO BE IN CONTROL!'

Does this scenario ring any bells for you? You're out on a dog walk when suddenly an unfamiliar dog, off-lead, appears as if from nowhere. An immediate deluge of anxious questions: What does it want? Where's its human? Is it safe? Does it want to play? Is that curiosity or aggression? Does it have a collar? Is it lost? Why is it coming towards us? Is it stalking us? Does it need help? How can I shoo it away, without communicating my fear to my dogs? On this last one, the ship has long sailed. Dogs are extremely sensitive to their humans' moods and our fear signals download quickly into them via their leads.

When this happened recently to me, the human eventually turned up and blithely shrugged 'nothing to worry about' before calling her dog to her side. This all took place in our newly adopted France and at such moments my French deserts me so it took me a moment to construct the line, 'You're supposed to be in control!' She waved this away, much as you would an irritating fly as she wandered on. My more articulate French friends have also challenged her and maybe something has sunk in because the last

'YOU ARE SUPPOSED TO BE IN CONTROL!'

time we met, her dog was on a lead. She ignored my conciliatory 'bonjour'.

Even before this second encounter, my fuming had been tempered by an awkward memory of a dog walk in the distant past. My newly adopted Lab Staffie cross was running around a car park, jumping up at windows to greet the occupants. His claws scratched the driver's door on a BMW. The driver yelled at me, 'You're supposed to be in control!' I apologised as I bundled him away.

The fact remains; we humans who take on canine companions must accept the duty of controlling them. If our dogs cause chaos, the responsibility lies with us not with them. They cannot be held to account for their actions as if they were humans. Our ancestors took them out of the wild, into the, unnatural-for-them human world which runs by rules they can never comprehend. That is why we have to be in control.

I often find myself wanting to say to God, 'You're supposed to be in control!' This comes when I am agitated about events in the world, i.e. quite often: the reckless killing of civilians, the rise of evidently dangerous populist leaders, the vastness of wealth inequality, the rape of the environment, the new wars that replace old wars, the industrialisation of animal abuse ... all of these alarm me and especially when supported by religious groups. How can God sit back and allow these things to happen? What is the point of being all powerful and then not using that power to prevent suffering? Isn't God supposed to be in control?

I do not expect a simple reply. I am hardly the first to level such an allegation at God. Job: 'Why do the wicked live on, growing old and increasing in power?'[130] Jeremiah: Why does the way of the guilty prosper?'[131] Habakkuk: 'Why do you look on the treacherous and are silent?'[132] There are answers of sorts but not sufficient to quench the questions. Maybe, with God, we are in the same situation as our dogs who will never understand all of *our* human ways of working. Maybe one day, in another life all will make sense. Until then, we mind our responsibilities, other humans abandoning theirs never lets

[130] Job 21:7,
[131] Jeremiah 12:1b
[132] Habakkuk 1:13

us off the hook. We pray, we trust, we protest, we lament, we give, we hope … and God … what does God do? This is impossible to answer but we do know that our honest cries, even the angriest and most accusatory ones will never drive God away from us.

Something to chew as your dog walks alongside you
Do I ever despair at God and God's seeming inaction? And then what? Where do I go next?

49

'YOU HAVE EVERYTHING YOU NEED! AND YET YOU STILL WANT MORE?'

Early one summer morning both dogs escaped. We had opened the door to the garden and they had gone out. After a while we realised that things were too quiet. We called, they did not come. They were gone. How? Presumably a new hole in the fence. But where? And which one had made it? And after all the money and effort we'd already spent on wire, boards and marquee pegs! And why was I wasting time on these thoughts when the only relevant question hung there unanswered; where were they? They could be anywhere ... they could be in danger ... they could be causing damage.

Where were they? We set off in different directions. There is no possibility of rest until that one question has been resolved. I barely noticed the new blooms, the birdsong, the bright chill in the air, the mist in the valley, the church bells chiming seven o'clock; these were an especial annoyance as they drowned my chance of catching a distant bark. Trying to panic-pray amidst sweating, panting and cursing, I jogged through empty streets calling their names, aiming at loud enough for them but not so loud as to awaken our neighbours; I didn't want word to get out that we have out-of-control dogs, a grave matter in a farming community.

Where were they? Twelve minutes had passed since I had realised they were gone. They've got name tags. They both carry my phone number. If they're found they will be returned ... if they haven't been shot first.

Sixteen minutes. The phone buzzed. Then the ringtone, the one allocated to my husband and to him alone. 'I've found them.' I ran to meet him ... and the dogs, both delighted with their adventure. It was bad. Dogs on the loose can do serious damage. What if they had caused a motorist to swerve and crash? What if they had cornered a cat? What if they had got into a field of cows? If you have a dog, you surely get the extreme seriousness of this last scenario? If you don't, please seek guidance at once; talk to more experienced guardians or better still a farmer. Pet dogs can never be allowed to harass livestock. It's rule 101.

Despite my panic, I had thought to pick up their leads before I'd left the house. And as we marched them home, I berated them, 'Why can't you be happy staying in the garden? Don't we give you enough? You have everything! Food! Exercise! Cuddles! Games! Warmth! Toys! Safety! You have everything you need! Everything! And yet you still want more?'

Some Martians were eavesdropping. One of them turned to God and said, 'Did we hear that right? One of your humans was upbraiding another Earthling for having everything and yet wanting more. Has irony died? Do they ever listen to themselves?' God smiled and said nothing. The Martians continued, 'Okay we know it's not all humans but it seems that those with the most are the least satisfied, never content, always eyeing the next toy in the shop.' God smiled again but this time the Martians wondered if the smile had become slightly rueful.

 Something to chew as your dog walks alongside you
How much energy do I devote to appreciating what I already have, compared with the energy I squander on craving new things?

50
'YOU'RE SO BRAVE … HIDING BEHIND THAT FENCE'

I once saw two dogs arguing ferociously with each other. They were on either side of a glass door, bouncing around with teeth bared. Then the smaller of the two, a corgi, called for time out. She strolled *around* the door, *past* the now calm retriever to a water bowl, took a drink then went back outside to her former spot and the two dogs resumed their fight.

Okay. When I say, 'I once saw …' what I mean is, there is a TikTok clip that frequently does the rounds. It's hilarious. Both dogs are clearly having the time of their lives, barking away at each other … but only when there's a barrier between them.[133]

When our dogs are having a merry old bark at any dog whose guardian has the audacity to walk them past our fence, I fantasise removing said fence and seeing if they would still be so fierce. I doubt it. The only time one of our dogs came face to face with the two local tearaways,[134] I dropped his lead and stepped back remembering

[133] Try searching YouTube with variations on 'Corgi vs Golden Retriever' and you'll find it!
[134] See chapter 45. Walks are work … wolf work (ii)

DOG LEADS TO GOD

an old lesson about how being on a lead affects a dog's behaviour in conflict. I called him back to me and with hackles raised he followed me home. There was some low-level growling but nothing like the racket made by our neighbours' dachshund ... from behind his fence.

We humans fight 'bravely' in much the same way, only our preferred 'barrier' is the internet. We can say appalling things to our opponents with an ease that we would never muster were we speaking in person. Keyboard warriors snarl viciously at each other when hiding behind false names and cartoon profile pictures. And get *so* angry.

Two of my previous bosses, both vicars each gave me a piece of invaluable advice. The first told me he refused to enter a written argument with anyone. If he received an unpleasant letter that deemed a response, he would ask for a meeting preferably over a cup of tea. The second had a mantra: discipline should always be at the lowest level possible; initial warnings gently offered with kindness, rather than summons to tribunals. Neither vicar ever imagined a slanging match on social media would lead to a positive resolution. Their way is harder and requires a deal more courage than rattling off tweets or barking through a glass door.

There is something far more wholesome, even healing about face to face encounters. Like dogs when the fence is removed, much of our bluster recedes when we meet in person either an adversary or someone we are keen to impress. God invites us to such an encounter, face-to-face and fence-free beginning in this life and then continuing onwards into the next. St Paul's great hope is for a day when we will be with God and we will know fully, even as we are fully known.[135] At that point both aggression and defences will become permanently redundant. There will be no hiding behind barriers or masks and no need to pretend to be anyone but ourselves because God will banish all our fears and finally reassure every hidden part of us that we are loved.

 Something to chew as your dog walks alongside you
Can I imagine an existence where all barking is only ever cheerful?

[135] 1 Corinthians 13:12

51
'I WEAR MY HEART ON A LEAD'

We are going to wander across that field again, where analogies are made between keeping a dog and having a baby, where people mutter 'child substitute' and not always with kindness. There are several links. Children and dogs are both completely dependent on us for more than mere food and shelter; we set their example. Neither small children nor dogs study moral law; their sense of right and wrong, acceptable and unacceptable comes solely from us: our words and more importantly our actions. And whereas children grow up and ideally leave the nest, our dogs remain with us for their whole lives. Consequently we embody their moral compass.

Elizabeth Stone has been widely quoted as saying, 'Making the decision to have a child – it is momentous. It is to decide forever to have your heart go walking around outside your body.'[136] Dog guardians will resonate with this. We too have repositioned our hearts. We wear our hearts on a lead. Which is often far from ideal; why did we ever think it wise to let our 'hearts' trot alongside us at litter level?

A man named only as 'Pete' was in agony following the theft of

---

[136] Quoted widely across the internet but sadly I cannot locate the original source.

DOG LEADS TO GOD

his car. His distress had nothing to do with his car (a silver BMW) and everything to do with his one-eyed, nine-year-old best friend, Bailey who was inside. Mercifully she was later found wandering in a town about half an hour's drive from the scene of the crime. Pete is clearly a man who wears his heart on a lead.[137]

When I worked as a prison chaplain, I would sometimes encounter new arrivals in a state of great torment, not primarily because they had been incarcerated but rather because their dog had been left home alone. The RSPCA once alerted would step in. I in turn would bring instant calm by returning to the wings with the news that the dog was now safe.

Two friends wore their hearts on an online lead. They were searching for a new dog. Their intention was to find one in their local rescue shelter but a stumble on the internet introduced them to Obie, a collie in Belarus! They fell in love with Obie before they had even met her and could not rest throughout all the long negotiations and journeying until she was finally safely in their arms.

If such love is considered folly then we are in good company, in fact we are in the best possible company. God's heart is placed in the most unsuitable and unlikely venues ... within us humans. This looks imprudent from without, as Paul notes, educated Greeks dismissed the Christian proclamation as 'foolishness' but he adds the rejoinder 'God's foolishness is wiser than human wisdom'.[138]

Love is risky. It is much safer to never love. C. S. Lewis warns us that loving anything, even an animal, makes us vulnerable; our hearts 'will certainly be wrung and possibly be broken'. The alternative, however, is playing it safe and never loving which consigns our hearts to an even greater tragedy, they become 'unbreakable, impenetrable, irredeemable'. Lewis ends with the sobering line: 'The only place outside Heaven where you can be perfectly safe from all the dangers and perturbations of love is Hell.'[139]

---

[137] 'Man reunited with one-eyed dog stolen in car theft', Susie Rack, Vic Minett, BBC News, bbc.com 24/04/2024
[138] 1 Corinthians 1:25
[139] *The Four Loves* by C. S. Lewis © copyright 1960 C. S. Lewis Pte Ltd. Extract used with permission.

'I WEAR MY HEART ON A LEAD'

 Something to chew as your dog walks alongside you
Do I keep my heart safely locked up ... or is part of it currently trotting along beside me, at the other end of the lead?

PART 8

TAIL ENDS

52
TAIL ENDS

In my other dog book (*The Dog Walker's Guide to God*), I lamented the Bible writers' lack of appreciation of dogs. Therefore I have taken my search elsewhere for quotable pro-dog thoughts. By 'elsewhere' I mean the internet, which can be wildly inaccurate and attribute random quotes to people who never said any such thing. I have tried my best to cross reference and verify but even so there may be errors. Here is what I found. To my relief, there are some important religious figures who *really* like dogs. Here are two quotes from Martin Luther:

> The dog is the most faithful of animals and would be much esteemed were it not so common. Our Lord God has made His greatest gifts the commonest.

> Be comforted, little dog, thou too in the Resurrection shall have a tail of gold.

There were also politicians: first Abraham Lincoln and then Woodrow Wilson, each employing dogs as a litmus test for a human's character:

DOG LEADS TO GOD

> I care not much for a man's religion whose dog and cat are not the better for it.

> If a dog does not come to you after looking you in the face, it is better that you go home and examine your conscience.

… and scientists: Charles Darwin states succinctly an observation many other dog guardians have made:

> It is scarcely possible to doubt that the love of man has become instinctive in the dog.

Two authors make a link between dogs and eternal bliss:

> Mark Twain: Heaven goes by favor. If it went by merit, you would stay out and your dog would go in.

> Milan Kundera: Dogs are our link to paradise. They don't know evil or jealousy or discontent. To sit with a dog on a hillside on a glorious afternoon is to be back in Eden, where doing nothing was not boring – it was peace.

Another author, gives a quote that I took as my motto while writing this book:

> Franz Kafka: All knowledge, the totality of all questions and answers, is contained in the dog.

And W. H. Auden notes dogs' boundless capacity for elation:

> In times of joy, all of us wished we possessed a tail we could wag.

The philosopher, Immanuel Kant makes a similar point as the US Presidents mentioned above:

> We can judge the heart of a man by his treatment of animals.

TAIL ENDS

The Ancient Greek Philosopher, Diogenes makes two dog points, one very good (if rather self-serving) and the second delightfully childish:

> Dogs and philosophers do the greatest good and get the fewest rewards.

> I pissed on the man who called me a dog. Why was he so surprised?

The 'man versus bear' debate went viral in 2024, as women answered the question 'Would you rather be stuck in the woods with a man or a bear?' Most women favoured 'bear'. Years before, Marilyn Monroe was thinking on similar lines when she said:

> Dogs never bite me. Just humans.

I'm glad to see such unexpected people rubbing shoulders, not least Darwin and Luther. Love can unite otherwise disparate people; love in all its forms, including human, Divine and by no means least, canine.

 Something to chew as your dog walks alongside you
When have I witnessed love bringing unlikely people together?

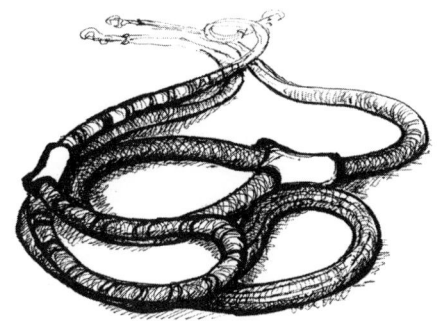

CONCLUSION

CAN OUR DOGS LEAD US TO GOD?

It seems so and not just for me. An author, an atheist and a priest all report some incredible spiritual stirrings within themselves when encountering these amazing creatures.

Dean Koontz the novelist, reports that stroking a dog soothes both heart and mind as much as deep meditation and benefits the human soul almost as much as prayer.

Ricky Gervais, the comedian well known for his outspoken atheism, says that the simple act of watching a dog is the closest he gets to spirituality.

Richard Rohr, Franciscan priest goes even further when he wrote :'Without any apology, lightweight theology, or fear of heresy, I can appropriately say that my black Labrador Venus was also Christ for me.'

I don't think I can top that.

Henry Martin,
Spring 2025

ACKNOWLEDGEMENTS

This book is dedicated to all those brave and generous souls who adopt elderly dogs. You are my heroes.

I did not intend to write a second dog book but then Hera arrived and I met so many other wonderful dogs and inspirational owners that I found myself unable to stop jotting down ideas.

My thanks go to:

David Moloney and all the team at DLT for placing such faith in me and my passions once again.

The C. S. Lewis Company Ltd and the Yearly Meeting of the Religious Society of Friends (Quakers) in Britain kindly permitted me to quote from (respectively) *The Four Loves* and *Advices & queries*.

My friends Anne El Safany, Guy Elsmore, John and Penny Applegate have generously given their time and insight to various drafts of the script.

The dogs who have been the models for some of my illustrations: Mr B, Louis, Nellie, Malcolm, Choupie, Georgie, Cooper, Shadow, Storm, Poppy, Truffs, Charlie, Oscar, Ruby, Lucy, Dobbie, Roo, Falba, Ted, Obie, Ronnie, Frank, Talisker, Archie, Lyla, Katie, Hugo and Hera.

I remain, as ever so grateful to Haydn, my husband and the love of my life. I still marvel that we have formed this little collective of four Hs.